The End Of The English

The European Superstate

An apology to my grandchildren

by

DAVID BROWN

The June Press

The Author

David Brown, is married with two children, one of whom is profoundly deaf and both brilliant. Former RN, RAF and pig breeder, and having had a farm in the mountains of Wales he is ably competent to be able to assess when politicians are lying to him. He has been researching the EU for some fifteen years. Some of his interests include the unlikely combination of being a dowser, a churchwarden, accumulating second hand books, planting orchards and a Fellow of the Linnean Society.

First published in 2008

by The June Press Ltd

UK distributor
The June Press Ltd
PO Box 119
Totnes
Devon TQ9 7WA
Tel: 44(0)8456 120 175
Fax: 44(0)8456 120 176
Email: info@junepress.com
Web: www.junepress.com

ISBN 978 0 9534697 6 5

This book is printed on environmentally friendly paper

Dedicated to my grandchildren Rona and Jane, and to my wife Ailsa for her patience and forbearance.

Contents

Acknowledgements

My thanks and gratitude go firstly to the many people who have given me the encouragement to write this book and expressed their eagerness to read it.

Their support has been a great encouragement in what has been a lonely task until this book finally came to life.

Secondly, my thanks to and admiration for all those dedicated "subversives" whose works and research form part of this book.

Particularly for their thoughts and ideas I am indebted to Matthew Brown, Keith Foster, Dr Rachel Hardie, Tommy Thompson, Tim Warren and my publishers the June Press. They have all been an invaluable weathervane on quality and presentation.

David Brown, 2008

Preface

Although dedicated to my two, this book is written for all our grandchildren, to try and explain how our generation let you all down and failed to keep a democratic self-governing country alive.

The idea came, my two will remember, when we were chatting at the dinner table, we adults and you two, Rona and Jane. In conversation we discussed how Parliament was elected and then we commented that the EU made most of our laws anyway and Jane aged seven asked "but who elects them?".

This seemed a good question deserving a proper answer and so I set to for a year to find one because it matters.

It matters because our generation will one day realise what they have lost, also because I care about you and I worry about your future.

In the process of writing I discovered how slowly and cleverly your freedom was taken from you and from us all.

My hope is that when you two are young adults your country will be free again and the European Union will have collapsed in tears due to its inherent contradications and people's thirst for freedom.

If this hope is realised then this book will be there for you and others to read so that you can understand the real story of how it happened.

Introduction

An increasing part of the population has never known a time when we were not either joined to the European Economic Community (EEC), or increasingly under the control of the European Union (EU).

There appears a need for a short readable but embracing account of how we arrived at the state we are in, what could be in store for us, and whether we can do anything about it.

It is aimed at those uneasy about the EU but lacking the factual knowledge to formulate that unease.

This then is about the politicians who willingly gave away our freedom and the many that couldn't be bothered or were too ignorant to care. Also about the relatively few of us who did realize what was happening and its consequences.

So how and why did we allow it to happen?

For years we wrote and remonstrated and put round leaflets and went to meetings, but with honorable exceptions we didn't fight heart and soul.

We all had lives to lead and families and jobs and all the day-to-day trivia of life to cope with. Anyway the British are naturally inhibited from making a public fuss and waving their arms about.

Crucially though, and this is true of the whole country, we had been a free people for so many centuries that we no longer properly valued it. We took it for granted and were not aware of the danger of losing it.

The progressive loss of freedom was harder to appreciate too because of the methods used by those who stole it. They always proceeded with small steps usually described as sensible economic measures and never to such a degree that would rouse revolutionary fervour and cries of "to the barricades".

Freedom went little by little, salami slicing, with a sauce of lies, half-truths and deception. Maybe we were all too comfortable and it was easier to believe the semi-lies and half-truths we were being fed by the media and our politicians and that once champion of liberty, the BBC.

The most potent reason though was treachery. This may seem now an unfashionable concept but when a country is betrayed by its own elected leaders, who people assume they can trust, then that country is in deep trouble.

But didn't somebody speak up? Where were all the revolutionary students? Well yes, quite a number did speak up but they were either ignored or rubbished.

In fact this year, as I write more and more people are discontented with the EU but not to the extent of starting a revolution at grass roots level. The prevailing mood seems to be apathy, that no one will listen anyway. With all the main political parties apparently happy to stay in the EU for a variety of their own reasons, that revolt looks distant.

There is a problem in presenting this book.

On the one hand the EU is such a vast and complex monster and I have accumulated so much material on it that I could easily bore the pants off people. I have therefore left out some complexities for the sake of clarity.

Further, it's difficult to make the loss of your freedom hilarious except perhaps in the chapter on "Lunacies". Also I have to admit I get so angry about it that sometimes it is difficult to present facts calmly and objectively, though I try.

Another problem in telling this story is the very effective tactic employed by those building the monster. This has been to make everything connected with it so complex, ambiguous and brain-numbingly tedious that ordinary people, and even the less stupid government ministers, give up and go and do something more edifying.

Finally, another complication is that as this process of our country's enmeshment goes on, what I write today may bear little relationship to our lives in ten year's time.

The EU by its very nature cannot stand still, and having no reverse gear, the direction can only be one way, and in the process more and more of our freedom vanishes.

Freedom is the one thing those who have lost it want above all else. It is desperately easy to lose and very hard to regain.

1

How it used to be

Sorry to take you back in history, but to realize how things have changed and what could be lost you need to know how things were and what must be protected.

Many countries still see the United Kingdom as the home of freedom with a unique system of parliamentary democracy based on the common law. Versions of this system thrive in the US, Australia and Canada.

My friend George Curtis suggests that the logic of power is that all rulers are robbers, all tax is theft and all politicians are potential tyrants. This perhaps sounds a little over-the-top until you think about it or until you start paying tax yourself.

He goes on to say that the relationship between the powerful and those over whom power is exercised determines whether you live in peace with one another in a state of relative prosperity, despite holding different opinions on nearly everything, or on the other hand in a state of frequent revolution or under tyranny.

The only nation in the world to have evolved the first and desirable of these two systems of government has been the English, with the Welsh, whose people have lived in peace with each other for over three hundred years. The Scots joined after 1745, then the Americans, apart from their civil war, and the Canadians, the Australians and the New Zealanders.

They all live under the protection of the law as free men.

The political life of free men rests on three things:
- the accountability of everyone in public life to the

electorate which can dismiss them.

- the rule of law, where a government may act according to the law or not at all.

- a free press and media, which compels politicians to respect the law.

Civil liberty, or freedom from enslavement, captivity, imprisonment or despotic rule rests on this rule of law. It is the most precious thing that any person can have and the only thing that all people, having lost it, will fight for above all else.

So what is our "Common Law?" It is "the will and custom of the people", a body of rights beyond the reach of Parliament. It is distinct from statute law, which is the will of Parliament and it cannot be repealed, only "improved" in modern parlance, though here lies the danger.

This body of rights, the common law, cannot be taken away by governments, for the people making laws have only the same rights as the people who elected them. The state answers to the people, not the people to the state.

It started with the Magna Carta in 1215 which gave crown recognition to long-standing Anglo–Saxon laws, rights and customs. It is a treaty or contract between the Crown and the people, not an act of parliament and again cannot be repealed by parliament, which it predates.

It was further strengthened by the Declaration of Rights 1688 and the Bill of Rights 1689, again a treaty or covenant between the crown and the people and it is renewed at every coronation for which reason, and because it is not statute law, it cannot be repealed.

These covenants clarified the way England should be governed in future based on self-evident freedoms existing by right and established so that any abolition of this framework would be illegal.

The first vital freedom these covenants enshrine is the right of Habeas Corpus, in that anyone accused once arrested must be taken to a public court within forty-eight hours and the evidence against them produced, or they must be set free.

Next is trial by jury which is the last safeguard against unjust law. Juries are more important than you can imagine for juries have the power, if they consider a law to be unjust, to set it aside and to ignore the direction of a judge.

This is why politicians loathe them. Juries are selected from the body of the people at random thus stopping selection by the government with obvious consequences.

Then there is the ancient rule of double jeopardy, where a defendant, once acquitted of a crime, cannot be tried for the same crime again. This prevents the prosecution persisting in retrials until they get a guilty verdict but this basic principle has been eroded by a British government decision to allow retrial where "fresh and compelling evidence subsequently arises".

The judicial process then is – (1) Suspicion, (2) Investigation, (3) Arrest, (4) Charge, and (5) Trial, and depending on the verdict, the sentence of the judge. The continental system is completely different, look up Corpus Juris in the index.

These safeguards ensure your freedom.

The way our democracy should work can be explained by one of the simpler definitions, in that a democracy is a state where the laws governing it are produced by the people elected to do so. This no longer applies.

You know all about Parliament, but forgive me, I'll spell it out again just to complete the picture. We have two Houses, the House of Commons and the House of Lords.

The Commons sits for a maximum of five years and then the government has to call an election. To put it bluntly, when we get fed up with the rascals we can kick them out and elect a new lot which is refreshing for everyone and inhibits complacency.

The various parties are restricted in what they can spend and how they spend it during the election campaign. The promises they make to get elected are gathered together to form their party manifesto.

Each MP represents a particular area called a constituency and the person who gets the most votes gets elected for the period of the government, by what is called the 'first past the post' system. The actual person elected, not just his party, can be held to account by his electors in their constituency.

The system of voting is by secret ballot, introduced in 1872, which with supervised polling stations eradicated widespread corruption.

The party which gets an overall majority of the seats is asked by the Queen to form her government. If no one party gets such a majority but has more MPs than any of its rivals, it can form a coalition with one of the other parties.

At the start of each parliamentary session the government puts together all it proposes to do in that session in a speech and the Queen has to read it out in the "Queen's speech" at a gathering of both Houses with what enthusiasm she can muster, whether or not she thinks it is a load of hogwash.

The purpose, if not the intention, of the second chamber, the House of Lords, is to stop the Commons in its tracks if it passes a law which is more than usually stupid or badly constructed or which the Lords consider unconstitutional or against the common good. It cannot kill a bill for ever, for the Commons being the elected chamber has the last word, but it can delay things long enough for second thoughts.

When the Commons gets completely frustrated by the Lords it can force through a bill by using the Parliament Act, for the House of Commons was supreme and made all our laws.

This Parliament Act is supposed only to be used in exceptional circumstances, though it is often abused by arrogant governments.

The Lords is an anachronism, and illogical, but in a curiously English way it works, or it does until restless reformers try and improve it for party advantage.

Its virtue, at least at present, is that it is a group of people who are generally fireproof and out of reach of party patronage and can think for themselves. They included until recently most of the hereditary peers collectively having a vast body of extraordinary knowledge and wisdom. However, most were sacked. In Parliament by comparison, many MPs have got very little experience of real life apart from going to school and getting elected.

The Lords also of course include a percentage of deadbeats promoted by the government of the day for loyal service to the party or it appears, particularly large donations.

At present it still has a few hereditary peers plus bishops and judges, but an increasing number of life peers, sent upstairs by a grateful government, are retired members of the new lifetime political class.

As I write, there is a mood to make it an elected house, which will guarantee constitutional chaos as generally happens when governments meddle with what already works reasonably well. Just for a start, an elected house would inevitably try and challenge Parliament as it would have the same basis of authority.

Here are a few more of the checks and balances which preserved our freedom (you will understand as you read on how it becomes more and more difficult to decide in which tense, past or present, to make such statements):

- there is the accountability of everyone in public life to the electorate because his/her tenure is only until the next election.

- this accountability has however been diluted by the vast expansion of QUANGOS, which translated mean Quasi Autonomous Non-Governmental Bodies which, though unelected, have accumulated vast powers over peoples' lives. Non-governmental is untrue as they are appointed and paid by the government; the only sense in which that is true is that they are unelected.

- to spell it out again, there is the rule of law, where a government can act only according to the law, or not at all. No one is above the law, all people are equal before the law and all are accountable. Judges and the judiciary are crown appointments and so free of politics, to the lasting irritation of politicians.

Another vital part of our freedom is a free press and television, however trivial and trashy parts of it appear.

There are continual attempts to restrict the ability of reporters not under government control to investigate what to governments, are sensitive matters, often by pressures not at once obvious. Unfortunately, over the past two decades parts of the media as well as other institutions have become politicized and are in many ways under the control of government, dependent on being fed favoured information. The media still appear on the surface generally representative of the whole spectrum of public opinion though sadly that is where the BBC often fails.

Also in this period governments have become dependent on powerful media interests and to a worrying degree influenced by them. Sadly, when I read or see on television something I happen to know about from personal experience it is often only half true or plain wrong. Wait until something you really know about becomes a news topic.

In spite of all its defects, Sir Winston Churchill, said "It has been said that democracy is the worst form of government except all the others that have been tried".

2

How it all began

Do not be too daunted, this is the simple version, grit your teeth and read on.

To understand how it all began it is necessary to understand the mindset behind the EU project and how they think.

It is summed up immaculately in a private letter, obviously not meant for publication, written by Jean Monnet, the French politician revered as one of the founding fathers of the EU.

He wrote – "Europe's nations should be guided towards a superstate without their people understanding what is happening. This can be accomplished by successive steps, each disguised as having an economic purpose, but which will eventually and irreversibly lead to federation".

Equally revealing is this address from Mark Leonard, from the 'Centre for European Reform':

"Europe's power is easy to miss. Like an invisible hand it operates through the shell of traditional political structures. The British House of Commons, the British Law Courts and British civil servants are still here but they have become agents of the EU implementing European Law. This is no accident. By creating common standards through national institutions, Europe can take over countries without necessarily becoming a target for hostility."

If you bear the advice of these two in mind then most of the actions of what was to become the EU become transparent and understandable.

As Janet Daley, a woman of luminous intelligence said, it should always be remembered that Europe does not have a deep commitment to democracy, at least not in the sense that the English speaking tradition understands it.

They do not share a reverence for the robustness of democratic institutions because in continental Europe democratic institutions have been anything but robust.

This is why the EU has been busily moving away from the idea of government being directly and transparently responsible to the popular will.

The terrible mass crimes of the 20th century and the collective guilt, which is still the motor force of European political consciousness, were all thought to have been generated or at least condoned by popular will.

Therefore, goes the thinking, the political instincts of the people are far too mercurial and inflammable to be trusted, or as Edward Heath our then Prime Minister famously said, "the British public are too stupid to be involved in governing themselves".

In addition the EU, you must remember, does not take any notice of what ordinary people think. The opinion polls they pay attention to are those which relate to TDMs, eurospeak for Top Decision Makers, at least those of them in favour of whatever the EU does.

Far better, the thinking goes, to leave the serious business of law-making to a professional class of administrators, an enlightened elite who will not be subject to the whims and passions of the mob which had brought such disgrace to their countries.

Democracy is all well and good in its place but the power of the people must be sieved, regulated and heavily supervised if it is to come to the right conclusion.

To accomplish this they set about creating a benign oligarchy though with no assurance to anyone that it would stay benign if thwarted.

This process began soon after the second world war, with the creation of the Coal and Steel Community which M. Monnet described as the first government of Europe.

The first major concrete step was the Treaty of Rome signed in 1957 which established the European Economic Community. This treaty was cobbled together in a chateau in Belgium by a body of politicians and bureaucrats. It was in effect a carve-up between France and Germany.

What was in fact signed in Rome with great symbolism was a pile of blank sheets of paper, except for the top and bottom sheets because the printer fell behind schedule.

They couldn't wait because they had to get it signed before Charles de Gaulle came to power in France, as he would have vetoed the whole idea. That signing of blank sheets of paper made the whole thing nonsense, didn't seem to worry anyone at the time.

In this Treaty, in Article 189, the *"acquis communitaire"* was established where no powers gained could ever be given back once the EU has gained what it calls competence over any community interest of any sort.

A little paranoia to flavour the story - what is now the Treaty of Rome bears a very strong resemblance to the plan developed by the monster Heydricht in Germany in 1942, called the Reich Plan for the Domination of Europe, for when Germany had won the war. The text bears remarkable comparison even to the dividing up of England into nine regions reporting, in this case, to Berlin rather than Brussels. Although widely circulated at the time copies of these proposals have now almost completely vanished.

Ashley Mote's book "Vigilance, a defence of British liberty" continues that in 1944, when the war was already lost, a secret conference of German industrialists and heads of the Nazi party was held in Strasbourg. They planned to hide away massive funds via Madrid to continue the fight to control Europe by stealth with a plan to cover decades ahead.

The theme of the meeting was "How will Germany dominate the peace when it loses the war" by creating a United States of Europe.

While we are deep in conspiracy theories it is worth having a quick look at the Bilderberg group.

The first meeting was called at the Bilderberg hotel in the Hague in 1954, chaired by Prince Bernhard of the Netherlands, a Nazi sympathizer. It included an unusual mix of bankers, industrialists, ex-communist agents and assorted government ministers. Often invited are younger politicians on the way up who it is considered may become powerful. It still meets yearly by invitation only at select locations, closely guarded by police and there is very seldom any media comment on it. No minutes are available and there is never any mention about what is discussed from those invited. Reports in the press are severely discouraged, which is easy if you are rich and powerful enough.

However a few year's back the annual meeting was held at the 5-star Turnberry Hotel in Scotland. Armed police and sniffer dogs turned the place into a fortress, roads were closed, bomb disposal experts checked delivery vans and marksmen patrolled the roof. The guests came mostly by private or official jets to Prestwick airport.

The official line is that the reason for all the secrecy is that the great and the good can speak freely without being quoted in the press. On the other hand one multi-billionare involved with the group thanked the media barons, in 1991, for keeping secret "our project for the world". He added "the multi–national sovereignty of an intellectual elite is surely preferable to the self-determination of nations as practised in the past".

One last quote from the very respectable *Financial Times* – "If the Bilderberg group is not a conspiracy of some sort, it is conducted in such a way as to give a remarkably good impression of one".

It may of course just be a crowd of very rich and important gentlemen having a yearly jolly but it might be worth keeping an eye on them.

There followed then, over the next three decades, a number of treaties named after the cities in which they were signed. Each one successively saw us lose more of our ability to govern ourselves, each giveaway shrouded in clouds of ambiguity. The Prime Minister at the time would trumpet some slight alteration as a great diplomatic victory for our interests to the home press.

It was well before we joined the EEC as it was then that the crucial Treaty of Rome was signed. In the 1960s the Common Agricultural Policy was launched and a merger treaty in 1965 created common institutions.

During this decade the UK tried twice to join what was then the EEC but was rejected by de Gaulle and the French, he rightly saying that Britain was maritime and insular and that her nature, structure and very situation differed profoundly from those of the continentals.

In the 1970s the disastrous Common Fisheries Policy was introduced as we finally joined with Ireland and Denmark. The Norwegians wisely decided to stay out.

We finally joined, throwing away control of our rich fishing industry as we did so, on the basis (as the PM Mr Heath said at the time) that the fishermen were politically insignificant and expendable. The Common Fisheries Policy came into being.

In 1975 the government called a national referendum on staying in the EEC on the basis of it being a free-trade area and who could disagree with that. Just so that they got the right answer every household had a fulsome booklet extolling staying in, plus the funding of a massive propaganda exercise with most of the press and of course the BBC promoting it. The few who fought against were rubbished and given no voice.

The British were not the only ones being lead up the garden path. The British Empire was essentially a trading conglomerate controlled by London which spread throughout the world. The system worked well and all the member nations tended to benefit in one way or another.

By the 1970s it had become sixteen nations forming the Commonwealth Realms, under the crown of the United Kingdom, with Australia, New Zealand and Canada as its principal members.

These sought assurances that "their interests would not be sacrificed for the sake of rehabilitating Western Europe", when it became clear that we were intent on entering an economic union with Europe. These assurances were readily given.

However the drive into Europe went ahead with little or no

consultation with the Realms who could sense a sell-out as well as anyone. They were therefore forced rapidly to find new markets, for at this time some 50 per cent of British trade was with the Commonwealth under preferential trading agreements and only about 15 per cent with Europe.

As a prominent Australian, Philip Benwell MBE said sadly in an address to the House of Lords, "Those of us who live outside Britain find it inconceivable that Britain would forsake a thousand years and more of constitutional and legal heritage to adopt continental systems that are not only alien, but repugnant to everything that Britain, its Empire and its Commonwealth once meant and was. To trade and legalise commercial arrangements through legal pacts are one thing, but to submit willingly to a full and total submersion into what will always be a foreign power is incomprehensible to say the least".

To resume our sorry tale, in the 1980s came the Single European Act which extended Qualified Majority Voting QMV. This, as it implies, enabled EU legislation to go through on a majority of votes, preventing the option of any country stopping something harmful to it.

There was also development towards European Monetary Union, the Euro, in the 1989 Delors report, and towards a Social Chapter which we initially avoided.

Greece, Spain and Portugal joined the club.

In the 1990s things really speeded up.

The Maastricht treaty of 1992 set up timetables for EMU, see above, and for European Political Union. It also created the EU, the European Union from the old EEC, the European Economic Community. You will forgive me using initals, you can appreciate the temptation.

To confuse the general public even more, the EU was set up in three pillars:

The European Community
Foreign and Security Policies
And Justice and Home Affairs

You can see it is getting some distance from a free-trade

area?

The Government, that is our government, under John Major then Prime Minister, forced the ratification of this treaty through parliament with every means in his power and just made it with a few votes to spare. Sadly it is easy for the party in power to bully MPs.

This was the occasion when Kenneth Clarke, a fervent supporter of the EU and then Home Secretary, admitted that he hadn't actually read the treaty or by implication understood it.

There then followed the Treaty of Amsterdam which extended QMV still further and added more provisions. We agreed to join the Social Chapter.

In 1999 widespread endemic fraud and mismanagement came to a head and the entire Commission who governed the EU resigned. Nothing much changed though.

Three more countries joined - Austria, Finland and Sweden. The Norwegians, after being asked to vote again, and this time get the right answer, again rejected joining.

Finally the common currency was introduced and eleven countries joined the Euro or the Eurine as some vulgar people called it. There were huge displays of fireworks and fanfares of self-congratulation and notes and coins came into use in 2002.

As Romano Prodi the Italian Prime Minister said in 1999: "The single market was the theme in the eighties, the single currency the theme in the nineties, we must now face the difficult task of moving towards a single economy, a single political unity".

There came next the Treaty of Nice in 2001; this dealt with the accession in 2004 of ten new countries, Greek Cyprus, Malta and eight from Eastern Europe, Poland, Hungary, Czech Republic, Slovakia, Slovenia, Lithuania, Latvia and Estonia. Each then had to set about translating the 97,000 pages of EU laws into their own language. Also the slightly sinister-sounding Eurojust was established.

In 2003 Mr Prodi's comments started to take shape when the draft constitution for the EU was finalized and discussed at the 2004 EU summit.

The way the treaty was arrived at was in the best traditions of the EU.

The theme was to bring Europe closer to the people. In practice, as with so much to do with the EU, they achieved the exact opposite.

It is worth repeating that all these treaties gave away more and more of our democratic liberties signed by ministers of the crown whose duty it was to protect those liberties and who had been given no authority to sign them away. They were basic liberties not for the disposal of any Parliament, only loaned to that body. At least until the threat of the EU constitution appeared, Parliament could repeal them.

This list of treaties though is only half the story. The reason the first treaty, the Treaty of Rome was so crucial were the profound changes in the effective context of the treaty as a result of so-called re–interpretation of the treaty by the European Court of "Justice".

The inverted commas on "Justice" are to make the point that the remit of this court is that all its decisions must further ever-closer union in the EU and some of its judges would not be recognized as such in England. It is in fact a political court, but as in any federal state, it has sole power over the scope and context of community law.

Among its judgments, in 1963 it decreed that "…. the community constitutes a new legal law for whose benefit the states have limited their sovereign rights….not only the member states but their nationals".

And in 1964 "….under the treaty, which carries with it a permanent limitation of their sovereign rights".

In 1970 it said that Community law should take precedence "over even the constitutional rights of member states … including entrenched law guaranteeing fundamental rights". By this did they mean Magna Carta and the English Common Law?

In case after case, although the treaty had not changed, its meaning had according to the court.

Even more serious, in 1992, in a ruling on the environment, the court took powers over a wide range of areas where it had other competence, i.e. control, to impose criminal offences and penalties.

As Martin Howe, QC says in effect, from this rolling process of re–interpretation it is apparent that no agreement or treaty defining EU powers can be safely relied on since they can be taken to mean what the court wants them to mean at any time in the future.

You may well have started wondering how the hell did they get away with it, taking over not just our country, but a whole continent?

In the UK the reasons were complex but with some very simple ones thrown in.

For one thing, there was an extraordinary level of ignorance among even quite senior politicians. As an example one minister thought the number of Directives imposed from Brussels in one year ran to a few hundreds when in fact it came to over four thousand.

Most important was that the politicians who agreed to and signed the treaties lied to us for thirty years. In many cases, great obvious whopping lies with a helping of just being economical with the truth. Classic examples were that of Mr Heath, then Prime Minister stating, when he was persuading us into joining the then EEC, that joining the then Common Market "involved no loss of essential sovereignty".

In old age he admitted with no shame that this was not true and that he was of course well aware that the eventual aim was a federal EU state.

Geoffrey Rippon, a minister in his government, when our fishery waters were being given away, said that "we retain full jurisdiction over the whole of our coastal waters up to twelve miles". This was a deliberate lie.

These deceptions were necessary for them because if they had spelled out the full implications of what they intended there might well have been a revolution.

The kindest way to account for this was that the more

honest ones were driven by a vision of a continent governed by an intelligent elite who of course knew far better what was best for "ordinary people" (that's you and me, your parents and all your friends).

In times past, simpler and more honest times, this was called treachery and dealt with appropriately.

A classic example of this is a Foreign Office paper written in 1972 and revealed under the thirty-year rule.

It deals with our entry into the then EEC and talks of "consequential weakening of national institutions and Parliament and that Parliament's last resort to assert a national interest and renounce a treaty is unlikely to be eroded in less than three decades....by then sovereignty.....would indeed be diminished". It goes on to emphasize that "it would be the major concern of Her Majesty's Government and all political parties not to exacerbate public concern by attributing unpopular measures or unfavourable economic developments to the remote and unmanageable Commission".

This serial mendacity, to use an elegant and comprehensive phrase, was restricted only to Britain. On the continent politicians were completely honest about their aims and plans.

A typical example was a quote by Joshka Fischer, the German foreign minister in 1998, who said "The top priority is to turn the EU into a single political state". This honesty could be an indication that what the people thought didn't matter in that democracy was a younger and less robust plant than in Britain. Also that at the beginning, at least, there was more support for the idea of ever-closer union for a variety of reasons such as anti-Americanism in France. Another major factor was greed.

Anthony Coughlan, a senior lecturer at Dublin University posed this same question of why? Why have Parliaments been so willing to divest themselves so radically of the power to make laws?

The answer seems to be that whereas at home they are subject to the restraints of democracy and the vote, in Brussels where laws are made primarily by the twenty-seven-member Council of Ministers, the national minister becomes a member of an oligarchy, the most powerful and unmovable community of lawmakers in history, making laws for five hundred million Europeans.

They become intoxicated with the increase in personal power as they act as supranational legislators.

As they increasingly "go native", keeping in with their fellow members of their exclusive club becomes more important than defending their people's interests. Dissent risks being branded as trouble makers. They come to regard the EU as giving them an exalted platform for their careers and their key function as being to deliver their national electorates to support EU integration.

When Ireland in a referendum rejected the Nice Treaty, their Prime Minister, Bertie Ahern, apologized profusely to his fellow heads of state for his people's delinquency and told them he would re-run the referendum and get the right result. That he did. This attitude of ministers then also frees national civil servants from scrutiny by their own parliaments and increases their power as they interact with their opposite numbers in Brussels on deciding EU legislation.

This aggravates the natural tendency of civil servants to pursue power and influence but now at supranational level.

Gradually the nation state is hollowed out, sucking the power out of traditional government institutions while keeping them formally in existence. They keep their old names, Parliament, Supreme Court so as not to upset ordinary citizens but their primary purpose now is to be transmitters of EU laws, edicts, legal judgments and directives.

Another factor was support from multi-national business, which could by-pass elected governments and deal with bureaucrats beyond democratic pressure and accountability.

Yet another factor was that if you employ bureaucratic gobbledegook to the level of a master's degree and include sufficient ambiguity so that it enables you to take your laws and directives to mean whatever you want them to mean, you can get away with anything.

This can even confuse the people who are producing the product. A Swedish economist, Maria Lindholm, reported that "one particular press release involving two Commissioners saw fifteen drafts and caused chaos". She added in a classic understatement that "The drafting of this text was not transparent for those directly involved".

Someone in Government had the incredibly optimistic idea that once people had read the proposed EU Draft Constitution they would fall in love with it and the EU office in London offered to send anyone who asked for it the whole document.

My own copy languishes yet on a shelf, all four hundred turgid pages of it and its a prime example of my point.

The EU has also employed for years a well tried and successful system of introducing complex legislation to suspicious and wary people.

Stage one - It is only a discussion document and it doesn't mean what its critics assert.

Stage two - It's only a suggestion.

Stage three - After a suitable pause, resignation, no point in complaining, it's all been agreed.

This way, new policies go from being unthinkable to being inevitable with no intervening stage.

Jeane Claude Juncker, the Prime Minister of Luxemburg put it succinctly. "We decide on something, put it out there and then wait for a while to see what happens. If no one kicks up a fuss – because most people don't understand what has been decided – we continue step by step until there is no turning back."

3

How it all fits together

There is an ancient saying in warfare, "know your enemy".

To stand any chance against the EU you need to know how it works, what drives the people who control it, who makes its laws, by what process and why lies and deceit are acceptable.

This last is rationalized by the naïve idealism of the EU dogma of "*la Pensée Unique*" – the only concept possible or the only way of thinking.

There persists in EU thought a pseudo-religious faith, a blind acceptance of the project, supposed to be pre-destined and therefore somehow sacrosanct.

The Vatican press office reported that the process of the canonisation of the three founding fathers of the EU had begun. One of the Vatican's supporters of this process of making them saints said that "the EU is a design not only of human beings but of God".

This religious endorsement explains why EU protagonists feel able to deceive if it furthers the EU project, a requirement for all utopian oligarchies.

To challenge the dogma becomes rather like questioning the existence of God. Paul van Buitenen one of the whistleblowers who tried to expose corruption was vilified as a "religious fanatic".

Thus any person or political party who questions the EU concept can be outlawed as a non-person or indeed a heretic.

The Advocate General at the European Court of Justice issued the chilling formal opinion that "criticism of the EU is akin to blasphemy and could be restricted without violating freedom of speech". This was part of the ECJ case C274/99P.

Our BBC adopted this doctrine whole-heartedly. The eleven

new countries joining the EU in 2006/7 were referred to as being anointed and the influential *Today* radio programme announced that the arrival of the Euro currency that the fathers of modern Europe dreamed about are all symbols made flesh. Perhaps as near real blasphemy as you can get.

The implication throughout is that the "sacred" ends justify any necessary means, whatever this involves.

So how does the system work?

Firstly there is The Council of Ministers, its president is the senior politician of the country whose turn it is and at present this changes every six months. Under the proposed draft Constitution there would be a permanent president.

At the top of the pile is the Presidency. The President of the Commission is appointed by the European Parliament. He has huge and almost limitless authority in guiding the Commission.

The President heads the European Commission, which produces and enforces all EU legislation.

It controls everything including the judiciary, the budget, legislation, the treaties and, in the words of Ruth Lea, is the "motor of integration". The commissioners are appointed (not elected) one from each country for a five year period and in our case are often failed politicians. They are assisted in producing the thousands of Directives and regulations by several thousand appointed committees whose make up is not revealed and whose actual existence is kept very quiet.

There follow six major institutions which also wield immense power.

The European Council:
This consists of the political heads of state, the President, another commissioner plus foreign ministers. This meets in secret, to work out foreign policy guidance and its interpretation.

The Council of Ministers:
This has the various foreign ministers plus the minister from each country who deals with the subject being discussed. In the

Council we have twenty nine votes out of three hundred and twenty one .

However, this body, the Council, is represented by a shadowy body which gets very little publicity called COREPER, the Committee of Permanent Representatives (i.e. member countries' ambassadors to the EU) which has enormous power.

It negotiates and approves the thousands upon thousands of laws from Brussels which are then proposed to the Commissioners. It meets several times a week and is in two parts, one which deals with regulations and business and a second part made up of ambassadors and bureaucrats, which deals with foreign policy and economics.

Neither is under any democratic control.

Next, and we have hardly begun yet:

The European Court of Justice:

This is responsible for the enforcement of Community Law and the supremacy of EU common law over national law. Its remit is that all its judgements must further the course of European integration.

The court is manned by judges from each member country some of whose competency would not be recognized in the United Kingdom.

There are also nine advocate generals who write opinions to influence the court's judgements. It also creates rights for EU citizens that national courts must enforce.

The Court of Auditors:

This acts as auditors for Community revenue and also external auditing of the institutions of the community. It should be a very important body as massive fraud is widespread. Unfortunately it is toothless as it has no powers to pass sentence, regain stolen funds or impose any sanctions. It has refused to pass the EU accounts now for the past thirteen years.

One of the EU's chief accountants drew attention to this and the totally inadequate system of accounting and was sacked by the then British commissioner, a certain Mr Kinnock, another failed politician who was in charge of investigating sleaze and fraud.

We are nearly there now:

The European Parliament:
It should be understood that from its inception the EU was designed to have what is politely called in Eurospeak a democratic deficit. However as there still existed a free if ill-informed press an impression had to be created of democracy and this led smoothly to the creation of the European Parliament. Members of this body are actually directly elected from each country, the numbers relating to the size of the country. They are elected by proportional representation (PR) to each party.

This means that the votes go to the party list and not individuals, so the party will choose who will become a Member of the European Parliament (MEP). This effectively rules out most independent people and none of them are accountable personally to the people who vote for them which is convenient.

More seriously, this lost ability to choose who should represent us, and the ability to hold them to account is one of the most important elements of political freedom. Further, the number of MEPs are allocated by large regions, of which more later.

We have just eleven per cent of the vote in the Parliament, seventy eight MEPs out of seven hundred and thirty two, and these are split between four parties.

They meet in a vast badly-designed building in Brussels, some seven hundred of them from all over Europe.

Except, to pacify the French, once a month the whole huge caravan, the papers alone in hundreds of lorries plus interpreters and all the other hangers-on trundle several hundred miles down to an identical building in Strasbourg.

Each MEP costs about one million pounds a year. Having found out that they were being overcharged on the rent by the City of Strasbourg because when the deal was done the Parliament didn't read the small print they decided to buy the vast complex for £96.5 million. However, there seems some doubt as to who owns the land upon which it stands so if they ever tried to sell it the whole edifice could revert to the landowner.

If you think this unbelievable, read on.

Each grouping of MEPs has a staff which gathers together and attempts to sort the huge amount of directives and regulations to be voted on and it is pretty dismal reading. The group then decides how much actual speaking time to allocate to each MEP. With the smaller groups perhaps ninety seconds in a week. The timing is absolute, go over your allocated time by two seconds and the microphone and interpreter are switched off, however vital your speech.

Since the MEPs have no power, hardly anyone apart from the interpreters listens anyway and for the same reason the press hardly bother. The chamber fills up at voting time, as, if an MEP is absent, he could lose 50 per cent of the daily allowance. They sit in numbered seats and place their smart cards in the electronic voting slots.

Everything the parliament votes on, every directive and regulation, comes from the Commission; they cannot originate legislation.

In the next hour they may be called on to vote up to two hundred times, often with very little idea of the reason or the result and what they vote on becomes EU law at once. The majority of British legislation now passes through this control factory.

As long ago as 2003 the regulations imposed on British citizens by the EU were probably in excess of two hundred thousand.

Nothing is ever voted down, and if by some aberration a vote was lost then the measure would go through a process called "conciliation" where the vote would be overturned and the original reinstated.

The whole thing is a mockery of the parliamentary process, a charade to provide the illusion of democracy. All these very expensive MEPs are merely bit-part actors, a veneer over a deeply undemocratic process.

As one English MEP put it, "we in Britain fought a bloody civil war and killed a king to be rid of such a system and to construct the delicate set of checks and balances which is the model for the world's democratic parliaments. Now we have rendered our parliament subject to a foreign absolute monarch".

Sadly though you will begin to understand that even these vast institutions are only part of the systems of control over your lives.

The Committee of the Regions.

This sounds like the usual boring organisation but far from it. It is fundamental to the EU project.

Europe is now split into some one hundred and eleven regions of between four and seven million people as decreed in 2003. The Council of Europe and a variety of regional associations have been working towards a "Europe of the Regions and the Cities" since as far back as 1950. The EU works long term.

My grandchildren's country Scotland, is still only an EU region even though by the time you read this it may on paper be independent. Wales and Northern Ireland are regions though they are allowed to keep their name.

England is a different matter. On one EU map, England vanished and was replaced by nine arbitrarily carved-up regions with no mention of traditional boundaries, counties or Westminster and Parliament. It could be worse I suppose, on another map they issued, Wales vanished into the sea and being a quarter Welsh I found this a bit extreme.

The reason for all this insanity is that the EU has always been planned long term to be a Continent of regions and not a Continent of nation states.

The long term plan is to break up the nation states and link each region to Brussels, legally and financially, by grants or more honestly bribes. To do this the regions eventually will bestride national boundaries thus diminishing national identity and control.

In 1996 a declaration of intent was signed by all the counties along the south coast, from Essex to Kent and Cornwall to agree to the founding aims of the Arc Manche region of Northern France whose capital is Paris. The Trans Manche regional website stated some years ago that the creation of regions crossing borders is part of the ongoing process of European integration and the removal of national boundaries.

The phrase "turkeys voting for Christmas" springs to mind but of course the answer is money, large sums are available as grants for projects as long as EU acknowledgement is splattered all over them.

In 1990 the EU Commission under the Interreg Community Initiative, adopted prepared border areas for a community without frontiers – "to ensure that national boundaries are not a barrier to balanced development and the integration of Europe". Even in Eurospeak that seems plain enough.

A bizarre German map shows the East coast of England joined with Scandinavia and the West coast of England with Western France and Portugal. One immediately thinks they are away with the fairies but remember the quotation of Mr Juncker, the Prime Minister of Luxemburg, in chapter two and it doesn't sound so funny.

The process started, as in most things to do with the EU, a long time ago. We were committed to setting up regional government when we joined the then EEC and signed the Treaty of Rome with its requirement to replace existing local government with regional economic government. Few people or politicians realized it at the time and those who did kept very quiet.

Even in 1963 before we joined up, ardent Europhiles, a useful group description for those who can see no wrong in anything to do with the EU, were planning eight councils in this country on a regional basis. Incidentally the opposite of a europhile is a eurorealist or eurosceptic of which I am one.

These boards consisted of civil servants, representatives of local authorities and selected people from business, the arts, charities and tourism who are today called "stakeholders", an EU term, but still unelected.

Successive governments have pushed on the process while still denying any EU connection. Any such question was met by the blank lie that "there is no community regional policy as such".

It would be remiss at this point, as one of the driving forces towards the regions, not to mention the Fabian Society. It is at the cutting edge of socialism in Britain and has been at the heart of the drive for a federal Europe since the First World War. Never heard of it, you may say? There are some two hundred Fabian MPs in the House of Commons. The society's approach is both subtle and clever and works mostly through front organizations and circles within circles. They do not seek publicity but they are very influential.

In 1974, under Prime Minister Heath, ancient cities and boroughs, urban and rural districts were swept away, aldermen were abolished, ancient charters and liberties and courts of record were all destroyed and incorporated into new unitary authorities which were in fact EEC sub regions. This upheaval was mostly to satisfy Britain's proposed EEC membership.

There followed several similar upheavals all to the same end which I won't weary you with but the pattern remained the same.

Coming nearly up to date in England a major step forward came with the government White Paper (a declaration of intent) with the title "Your region, your choice". This last bit it most certainly wasn't.

This was a document full of verbiage such as "economic cohesion", "joined up government" and "real knowledge" included in a mixture of contradictions, dubious logic and repetition. It also had a sprinkling of EU-speak which betrayed its origins such as "spatial planning" and "concordat" and the repeated use of the word "devolution".

When the chaff was blown away the real plan appeared. It was firstly to move some government offices away from the capital to regional centres.

Secondly, to move more and more powers away from the established county councils to the regions. The White Paper failed to mention that the powers being given to the regional assemblies were powers already ceded to Brussels.

The third necessary stage was to be the abolition of county councils.

Already a wide range of power and powers had been transferred to the regions. In addition Government offices in the regions were already carrying on the work of many Whitehall departments. It would be very easy to transfer these departments to the regional assemblies.

Fire and Rescue were planned to be organized from county to regional level, 48 control centres becoming regional ones at huge expense. If there is one thing you need in a fire service it is rapid response and local knowledge but if it is an EU command, common sense takes second place.

There was an attempt to change the county police forces to huge regional ones but not all chief constables had yet been made politically compliant and there was widespread and well-publicized resistance and this appears to have gone on the back burner. However as you have seen, the EU knows how to wait. The job of pushing forward the regional assemblies was passed to John Prescott, then deputy Prime Minister who claimed it was all his idea. Although his department, which had huge powers, continued to try and pass powers to the regions, such as putting the fire services on a regional basis and control of planning, he over-reached himself by proposing a referendum for the NE region (which was strongly pro-government) on having an elected assembly. They were so sure of the result that they signed a lease on a large and expensive building to house the new assembly. You will notice that the referendum was not whether to have a regional assembly at all, just whether it should be elected. Over 70 per cent of the electorate voted against it and like the EU, the government rapidly learnt its lesson and there has been no hint of asking the electorate their opinion again.

Again like the EU, when the people say no, it is continuing to increase the power of the regions by stealth.

Eventually the government bowed to a combination of mockery and argument and announced in 2007 that the Regional Assemblies would be abolished by 2010. This sounded a little too good to be true and in fact most of the powers the Assemblies have gained will be passed, not back to the elected county councils but to the Regional Development Authorities, RDAs, originally set up in 1999. These are in fact totally government-controlled Quangos with just as much power as the reviled Assemblies.

Which brings us again to Quangos, already mentioned in Chapter One. These, to remind you, are Quasi-autonomous-non-governmental bodies. Non-governmental is being slightly economical with the truth, as these are paid for by the taxpayer and appointed by the government.

They nearly all have a political agenda but are outside all democratic control or accountability. Many are filled by a new class of bureaucrats mainly owing their livelihood to their political party. Their number, cost and subtle control of our lives has increased year by year and in 2007 the government admitted their yearly cost as an incredible £167 million.

Lobby Groups:

Another way the system works is by the formation and use of lobby groups. There is a huge swathe of ten thousand lobby groups covering the whole of Europe, financed by taxpayers' money, in 2007 it amounted to eight hundred million pounds a year. They are employed to create the impression of wide-ranging debate with independent groups and, strange though it may seem, the Commission having created them uses them to lobby itself. The Environment Commissioner, Stavros Dimas says this is to remedy Europe's "democratic deficit".

There are a host of them, going under acronyms, CoR, ECOSOC, CALRE, REGLEG, AEBR, CEMR, AEBR, CEMR,

AER, CRPM, to quote some of the bigger ones. Even the British government has copied the system; it has lobbied itself on regional government using groups it pays to ask the right questions.

Just one of the EU groups, the Committee of the Regions (CoR), gives opinions on and is consulted as representing 85,000 local and regional authorities. The 317 CoR members act only in the interests of the EU, not the people they purport to represent.

Like many other EU organizations, the CoR has been exposed as being plagued with fraud.

Its internal auditor, Robert McCoy, exposed this time and again but in usual EU fashion he was blocked at every turn, even though the EU parliament actually supported him. He was eventually forced out and retired a broken man, a not unusual fate for EU whistleblowers.

Another well-organized way of promoting "the project" is plain old fashioned bribery. It's not called that of course but the beauty of it is that countries are bribed with their own money. The money comes in the form of grants for EU projects which are funnelled only through the regions and since 1960 when the first EEC Structural Fund was set up they have proved very attractive.

It provokes most local authorities to set up European departments to promote the EU and qualify them to get back some of the British taxpayers' money already paid to Brussels.

Even better, by EU law, to get grants all regions must set up an office in Brussels and have direct contact with the EU Commission.

There are over thirty UK offices in Brussels, many costing up to a million pounds a year to run. None of the British regions have an office in London, their national capital. The new British capital is Brussels.

Remember, all this tedious stuff is but a fraction of the whole story but you will, I hope, now have a general background impression of the system which has taken over your country and you can better judge the pixie dust with which your politicians try to blind you.

4

Resultant lunacies

Many books and an immense acreage of newsprint have been devoted to the appalling but inevitable consequences of laws passed by remote bureaucrats. The dreadful years of the Soviet Union are a chilling example but the EU system is running it a close second.

This system is made infinitely worse by the impulsion to apply laws indiscriminately to a huge and diverse continent of nations all speaking different languages.

Add to this the turgid gobbledygook in which so many of them are drafted and their dreary length.

A large proportion of the problems arise from or come under the heading of "the law of unexpected consequences" due to the Commission's touching belief that "one law will cover all the complexities of life on a continent of several hundred million people".

In addition, directives are often gold-plated by our home-grown bureaucrats in Whitehall if only to justify their existence, which make their effect even more onerous.

"The Mad Officials" by Booker and North identified the six point sequence where, in their words, the machine goes off the rails.

These were:
1   The EU factor and the flood of directives from Brussels which you are beginning to be familiar with having got this far.
2   The Whitehall effect, when the regulations were put into British law often making them far more damaging.
3   Home-made regulatory law as a result of EU Directives,

such as the Children Act 1989.

4   The enforcing of guidance on EU law as if it was actual law and which was in fact beyond the law.

5   Overzealous enforcement and the puritanical aggressive zeal with which officials treat the public, almost on the assumption that they are criminals. Civility and common sense are often missing.

6   The resultant climate of fear and confusion with the mass of new regulations and the increase in official powers making people afraid to challenge officials or their demands.

Getting back to the root cause of it all, EU directives can be sub–divided into a number of categories. Many are, if one is feeling charitable, well-intentioned but it is the result we are concerned with. Let us bear in mind the well-known saying, at least well-known to your grandfather's generation about "the road to hell being paved with good intentions", and stop feeling charitable. Many of these examples are the work of the sterling Messrs Booker and North which at least ensures the jobs of a number of Brussels bureaucrats employed in sticking pins in their effigys.

1   Those laws which put huge unnecessary costs on thriving businesses which often make it impossible for them to survive, of which there are some thousands.

2   Those which just make life for the ordinary citizen more irritating and, as a bonus, add to the control of officials over our lives.

3   The directives which impose monstrous costs on the whole country and thus the taxpayer, often running into billions of pounds sterling.

4   Laws where they prohibit or destroy ancient and harmless customs, often involving social or political engineering.

5   The completely lunatic.
6   The possibly well-intentioned in a blundering sort of way but subject to the law of unexpected consequences.

In the words of Vladimir Bukovsky, a Russian dissident of many years bitter experience, "….the results of what they are trying to do in Europe will be the exact opposite of what they promise. This always happens with socialist utopias, they ignore human nature, they want to change it and when it bounces back they are all surprised".

The huge regulatory explosion which now afflicts us originated in large part from acts of parliament, put into law because we had to implement various EU Directives. Here are some of them.

The Health and Safety at Work etc Act. 1974
The Financial Services Act, 1986
The Children Act 1989
The Community Care Act 1990
The Environmental Protection Act 1990
The Food and Safety Act 1990
The Fresh Meat Regulations (Hygiene and Inspection) 1992
The Vehicle Excise Duty (Reduced Pollution) (Amendment)
The Data Protection Act
Control of Asbestos at Work
Disability Discrimination (Providers of Services)
(Adjustments from 1999 of Premises) Regulations 2004.

Each of these acts subsequently gave birth to a mass of subsidiary regulations implementing further EEC/EU directives and this is ongoing. To take just one example the Animal by-products regulation 2003 which came from EU regulation 1774/2002 puts more than five hundred new criminal offences on the statute book, each punishable by a fine of up to £20,000 or two years in prison.

My favorite example of officialdom is the visit of a Health

and Safety officer to a Welsh farm show who insisted that a completely open tented lean-to must have a fire door. This must come under category 5, and when I analyzed some of the thousands of examples of EU directives and their results, surprise, surprise, category 5 came out way ahead. For this reason, there may follow a few extra of these and anyway they are more entertaining.

Also I had originally included a category 7, as a category including elements of the preceding six but as this seemed to cover most of them I left it out.

So, a few examples in each category, which makes for hard choices given the number available.

Under category 1, costs on business:

A small Welsh Fresh Meat Company in 1992 had to cease trading and, at a cost of £20,000, raise its ceilings by six feet.

Under the Environmental Protection Act 1990, the Health and Safety Executive decided that petrol tanks had to be leakage tested by filling with water instead of by inert gas as before. The tank is thus contaminated and huge amounts of now polluted water must be taken often for long journeys and always expensively by an "authorized contractor" to a designated site.

The bizarre Physical Agents Directive on Vibration in 2002 affects practically every human economic activity connected with machinery. An arcane formula measures vibration in metres/second squared and restricts each machinery use under strict time limits. Initially a tractor driver would be limited to three hours, a lorry driver to six and so on down to chain saws. Costs of inspection of each tool or vehicle could be up to £1,000. The cost to British industry is estimated in £ billions. The storm of protest got some of the limits eased and the enforcement delayed until 2007. It also threatened to close down the British Army as tanks tend to vibrate a bit when in action.

Some twenty five firms used to convert cars so they were accessible for wheelchairs. An EU directive has reduced the number of vehicles from each model which can be converted from 500 to 75, making the whole process uneconomic. The head of the Commission Automotive Unit said he could do nothing to help.

The EU directives 97/67 EC and 2002/39 were designed to break up postal monopolies. Postcom set up under EU rules, has imposed crippling losses on Royal Mail, which is handicapped in that by law it is required to deliver mail to anywhere in the UK for a fixed price.

Royal Mail's only solution has been to drastically raise the price of first and second class stamps. Further, although the government has been allowed to continue subsidizing small post offices by £150 million a year it is forbidden to increase this. As inflation takes its toll the post offices go out of business, 2,500 in 2006/7, causing distress to many old people in rural areas, apart from the owners of the post offices. The government has helped their decline by taking away services from Post Offices.

You do realize why I keep putting in the numbers of the directives which more and more rule our lives?

Firstly it's to show you that I'm not making it all up but also to show you the mind-boggling extent and intrusive pettiness of this vast bureaucracy.

To resume. - There was a creamery on the west coast of Scotland. The waste water went out to sea, was perfectly harmless and provided nutrients for fish. Under the EU's waste water directive the supplying farmers were asked for £1.2 million pounds to take the water further out to sea which would bankrupt them and the creamery. In Islay in a similar case the creamery closed, the cows were shot and the farmers had to pay to have the carcasses shipped to the mainland for incineration. In Brussels the sewage produced by the officials who wrote the directive goes straight into the North Sea.

This section could go on and on but that's enough to give you a flavour.

Category 2, irritating and distressing to the citizen:

The EU Directive on Heights even influences changing a light bulb in a church. This used to be done by sending a volunteer up a ladder. Instead, scaffolding must now be used and the cost has risen from nil to a possible two day job and £1,500. Further, acrobats in a visiting Russian circus were told they had to wear hard hats.

Local fishermen were fined £300 for selling lobsters 86mm long. The EU demand that only lobsters 87mm long may be caught.

Not yet a directive but rest assured it won't be long, the EU Transport Commissioner in 2007 plans legislation to make all cars run with their lights on permanently. This is more one-size-fits-all thinking, because Scandinavians with their murky winters need it so must we all. It will, of course, increase fuel use and exhaust fumes.

A large white van was seen touring Yorkshire plastered with signs asking "Can't make sense of legislation?" and a red tape hotline number. On the back a ring of stars and "sponsored by the EU".

When the Italians had their man as the six-month EU president they worked hard to get a directive to abandon the hallmarking of silver employed in Britain for centuries and which guarantees quality. The Italians have a very large trade in silver jewelry.

A cheerfully outspoken Yorkshire farmer bought a few hundred tons of builder's rubble to repair his farm roads. He was rung up, spoken to like a criminal and threatened with prosecution under EU legislation for running an unlicensed waste site. The head of the environment agency then claimed he had illegally dumped 100 tons of asbestos. Investigation showed no asbestos and the case was dropped.

The Meat Hygiene Service, part of the Food Standards Agency, employs 2,250 officials to enforce regulations on some 1,300 licensed meat premises. Since the only places needing frequent visits are the 300 slaughter houses left, this means about six officials per unit.

However Danish farmers are even better looked after, they have 29,000 officials for 29,000 farmers.

Category 3, monstrous national costs:

Britain opted out of the Working Time Directive in the Maastricht Treaty, but the EU enforced it on us subsequently as a Health and Safety measure. It forces people to work no more than 48 hours per week and no more than 11 hours in any one day. A better way to stifle enterprise and initiative has yet to be devised. Our own government estimates that it is costing 1.5 to 2 billion pounds per year. There was originally exemption for some particular jobs but this was later removed.

The Common Agriculture Policy, dreamed up to protect French farmers before we even joined the community, takes up nearly half the EU budget making farmers servants of the state and resulting in surpluses dumped on third world countries which ruin their farming industries. To avoid this, farmers are now paid not to grow food with their every move spied on by satellites and their time taken up by an avalanche of paperwork. It also makes our food unduly expensive.

Under the New EU Single Farms Payment scheme the system to deliver payments was made so complicated that a complete shambles ensued within DEFRA, so much so that it cost £500 million, £305 million of which was in the form of fines paid to Brussels for being late, instead of going to the desperate farmers who were put in hock to their banks because of the delay in payments.

The utter futility of the EU directive to the UK to produce 10 per cent of electricity from renewable sources by 2010 cannot be better shown than the plan to build 181 giant wind turbines over 400 feet high on the beautiful and remote Isle of Lewis in the outer Hebrides to produce uncertain quantities of very expensive electricity.

Their rated capacity is 650MW, equal to a small conventional power station. The best it will achieve will be around 200MW of which 80MW will be lost in transit and then only when the wind is blowing at the right speed. Meanwhile conventional power stations are needed to be on stand-by when the wind fails. These monsters are being imposed on people right across the country by government inspectors in spite of ferocious opposition from local councils and MPs.

There have been three EU Water Purification Directives. Spending to comply with these directives to date has achieved the remarkable total of £65 billion. Although a very worthy idea, the requirements have been often absurdly over the top including £3 billion on de–nitrification plants to remedy a problem which after more research turned out not to exist. Work on flood prevention was cut to the bone to coincide with nationwide floods in 2007, partly to save some of the money paid to Brussels in fines for slow payment of farm grants.

HACCP, pronounced Hassup, stands for Hazard Analysis and Critical Control Points. This was the system devised in the United States to produce zero risk food for astronauts.

The EU decided with peerless logic to impose this system on all food premises in the EU including the UK.

It involves ticking complicated boxes which once ticked then can be forgotten as can be common sense and observation.

Just one example, a butcher or chef is sent on a course on Hazard Analysis which must be done on every action or part of a menu in a restaurant, taken by a lecturer who may or may not fully understand food safety, and they are then given a four volume manual to tell them what to do. The nightmarish complications could well put back food safety for years.

The Draft Soils Directive, to implement the EU's soil strategy, which few people knew they had acquired. Any buyers of land must be told all past activities on the site, and member states are required to identify soil protection "priority areas" and take "appropriate measures" to protect against erosion, biodiversity loss and other threats. It will increase administrative burdens on member states, authorities, vastly increase bureaucracy and completely ignores the already farcical EU objectives of better regulation and simplification. We now have a Single European Soil.

Category 4, spoiling ancient and harmless activities:

Under the Directive on Rail Safety, Heritage steam train lines which never go faster than 25mph and are run by volunteers come under the same law as high speed main lines. This involves having to pay for rail inspectors at £200 per hour which they can't afford and resulting in possible closure.

A really effective way to clear ponds and water courses which has been used for centuries is to put barley straw in the water. Not any more. Under the European Biocidal Products Directive barley straw must be treated as a brand new pesticide needing two years of very expensive testing. A company which was selling hundreds of thousands of small barley straw mats for garden ponds has had to stop, so people now have to use pesticides.

Category 5, the completely lunatic:

One of Mr Booker's stories in the *Sunday Telegraph* details how a leading firm of makers of false teeth was struggling to fill in a Eurostat prodcom survey intended to itemise community products. Finding no entry for dentures the nearest relevant box was food processing machinery. They are now classed as the country's largest manufacturer in this class.

Farmers and stock owners may no longer keep a muck-heap weighing more than five tons without a licence costing between £100 and £500, plus the cost of weighing the heap.

Converting of old buildings, derelict mills and buildings on industrial sites with government financial grants has been forbidden by the Brussels Competition Commissioner as "illegal state aid".

A lady who cooked for a local pub, the Bateman Arms in Herefordshire, baked, "Red Dragon Pies" because they contained Chinese aduki beans which give you the strength of a dragon. A trading standards officer called and solemnly told her that if they did not contain dragon meat she could not call them Red Dragon Pies. She was relieved to hear that her cottage pies and shepherds' pies were exempt from the Trades Descriptions Act.

Under the Human Rights Act the Lord Chancellors Department ruled that prisoners in court must no longer be seen to be in handcuffs as this equated to torture under the act. The result has been the closure of many smaller courts due to the crippling cost of complying with the act, causing hardship and delay in justice with people having to travel long distances to larger courts.

Waste bread at the bakers used to be given away for feed for animals and chickens. Now it is classified as hazardous waste, and an expensive licence is compulsory to transport it to a registered site. A charity though, presumably with a licence, can collect the bread for animals. The Act applies also to a painter who can take a full can of paint on to a job but the empty tin is hazardous waste.

On the land of a Cumbrian farmer a rambler found the skin of a dead lamb. As any countryman knows, the skin of a dead lamb is often put on an orphan lamb so that its foster mother will accept it. The rambler reported the find to the police and in the next two weeks the farmer had visits from the following:

The police and the RSPCA (potential cruelty)
Environmental Health (public health risk)
The Department of Agriculture
The Countryside Commission
Cumbria County Council, (disposal of hazardous waste)
The Ramblers Association, (hazards on footpaths)
Two departments of the Environment Agency (pollution of water courses)
The Parish Council
Local Planning Authority (change of use to an unauthorized slaughter house)
And Cumbria Social Services (possible satanic abuse)

In his spare time he looked after his livestock.

The EU sent several hundred people to police the elections in the Congo. Some just hung around the airport, some of them ended up in a totally different country called Gabon with a coastline of 10 to 15 miles and quite a few stayed in Germany. The operating instructions for this operation included that EUFOR submarines are not required to navigate on the surface and to show their flag in the territorial sea of the host state. This one is included to show how the EU is quite impartial in how it works all over the world.

EU Directive 2000/13 makes it a criminal offence to sell any food, human or animal with more than 0.9 per cent of genetically modified ingredients. No government body, including the Food Standards Agency, has the ability to measure this requirement and there is no way to enforce it though it is now passed into law.

New members of the EU, Malta and Cyprus, can now nominate well-paid members to the new EU Railway Agency.

Neither country has any railway. Luxemburg and Austria help decide the Common Fisheries Policy which controls access to Britain's fishing waters containing 80 per cent of Europe's fish. Neither country has any coastline or a single fishing boat.

A Cambridgeshire farmer ploughed through three booklets and 42 pages from the Environment Agency on disposal of agricultural waste. He discovered that to dig out a ditch, to avoid paying for a licence for waste management and a fee of £20,000, he must opt for an exemption.

In this it states that all ditch material must be spread on the bank only, or a fine of up to £5,000 will be levied. However, DEFRA states that any material placed nearer than two metres to the ditch is an offence under "cross-compliance rules" where he could lose part of his subsidies.

Category 6, the law of unexpected consequences:

Because under the Common Agricultural Policy farmers had been paid billions of pounds to overproduce, the natural results were beef and grain mountains and wine and milk lakes. The EU then set quotas for milk production. Britain, once self sufficient in milk, now has to import millions of pounds worth a year. Apart from driving farmers out of milk production this especially hit a specialist cheese producer who only made cheese from milk from his own cows. After five years of reduced cheese output he was given a cheque for £200,000 for cheese he had never made.

Makers of model railway engines are being closed down by the European Pressure Equipment Directive, designed for the control of huge boilers in factories. Now the tiny boilers on model engines must be inspected at a cost of £700 per day. In any event model trains use copper for their boilers which implode rather than explode under pressure.

The End of Life Vehicle Directive in 2002 decreed that old vehicles can no longer be scrunched up and melted down but dismantled at special sites and their components recycled. Very worthy but the result is large numbers of old cars abandoned or burnt out due to the cost of disposing of them. The same thing happened with a similar directive on old fridges and freezers under WEEE, the Waste Electrical and Electronic Equipment Directive. The foreseeable result was fields full of old fridges, especially as there was not one recycling plant in the country.

The Common Fisheries Policy, which needs a book on its own, requires the dumping back in the sea of hundreds of thousands of tons of dead fish every year if the nets drawn through the sea were unintelligent enough to catch fish for which the boat had no quota. This has resulted in a near-terminal decline in fish in the North Sea and the ruthless enforcement of the policy in Britain has brought the approaching destruction of a great fishing fleet.

The Scilly Isles helicopter service came under grave danger with EU regulation 295/91 which said that any passenger who was unable to fly when booked could claim £750 compensation. This was bearable for transatlantic flights but would have bankrupted this small but essential service. Unusually, officialdom relented and the charge was altered for the Scilly Isles.

The EU has made it compulsory from 2009 to use low energy light bulbs, or compact fluorescent lamps. If broken they spill mercury which is highly toxic and assuredly comes under an armful of directives. Further, unless they are left on all the time, they don't save power due to the high energy needed for start up. No one, certainly not the EU, has any idea where to put the eventual billions of discarded toxic bulbs from 2009 on.

Since the power to regulate waste management was given to Brussels an avalanche of EU directives has fallen from above making it harder and harder to dispose legally of all sorts of hitherto legal waste. Further, the definition of hazardous waste has been tightened to a farcical degree. As night follows day this has resulted in a plague of fly tipping and this will get worse as we head towards 2010 and our 182 landfill sites for "hazardous waste" are reduced to 14. This means, according to the EU Environment Agency, twenty seven million tons moved to other forms of waste disposal.

The government's solution is 165 giant incinerators which it will have to force on an unwilling country. Meanwhile in the short term, the government has made farmers responsible for waste dumped on their own land which is neat but contemptible.

Enough of this nonsense for now. Perhaps you can now begin to see how the EU attempts and in many ways succeeds in controlling and permeating every aspect of your lives. This control is seldom blatant and often not even apparent. This is partly because very few of the laws enacted by what passes for our national government acknowledge their true EU origin.

The core reason for the sad results and chaos caused by this flood of regulation is that the Commission officers who draft them have very seldom actually worked in or had any experience in the industries they are controlling. Being politically appointed, they lack competence and know-how in industry. The only people consulted are some multi-national organizations which can sometimes influence Commission decisions detrimental to small businesses.

Believe me that this is a very small but reasonably representative sample.

5

How we are controlled

We are controlled in these interesting times of 2008 to an unprecedented degree in what we think, what we do and what we say.

The methods used to achieve this degree of control can be put loosely under the following headings:

Firstly and most importantly is the control of people's thinking, which is achieved by a long-term barrage of information or mis-information: in effect, propaganda.

Having the same effect is that bane of free speech, political correctness which we all used to laugh about.

It is in danger of becoming a means by which a vocal minority can inflict their views on a complacent majority. The result is the closing down of rational adult debate on a number of no go subjects, and where eventually only one view is tolerated.

The next is by information control technology which is now available to enable a government to know everything about you and to have that information at its fingertips. By this I mean ID cards and the growth of massive data bases with practically unlimited storage capacity.

The third way is by spreading the feeling of fear, of terrorism or any external threat so that we don't make too much fuss when new laws further restrict our freedom. We are also inhibited in what we say by the growth of political correctness which spreads like a fog through social intercourse. It becomes a form of self-inflicted censorship which would be ludicrous were it not so dangerous.

Finally there is physical control, by officials who are entitled to enter your home or stop you in the street or close off areas of a town for plausible reasons. Under this heading comes the huge growth of CCTV, speed cameras and, road pricing projects needing the installation of sensors in your car - and this is just the beginning.

So far in this country this has not been a big issue but read on to see the possibilities. Still more or less outside our borders is Europol, the EU police force and an incipient EU paramilitary police force.

Before we start looking at control by the EU, or "Federalist Thought Control" as the Bruges Group eloquently puts it, let us look at a few definitions of propaganda.

The most chilling one perhaps is "to describe attempts by a totalitarian regime to achieve comprehensive subordination of knowledge to state policy".

A 1946 definition suggested the difference between education and propaganda was that the former dealt with uncontroversial matters while propaganda relates to controversial issues.

A 1992 one said it involves mass suggestion, the manipulation of symbols and the individual's psychology.

In 1999 a further report suggested that propaganda has a clear coherent purposive ideology, even utopianism. It ignores argumentative exchange and there is seldom any element of give and take.

The application of these definitions to examples of EU "publicity" in this chapter illustrate the extent of the problem.

Firstly though what are the UK government rules on public information campaigns conducted by the civil service. They sound eminently sensible and just.

To summarize, resources may not be used for party political purposes, they should only deal with matters where the government has direct responsibility, information should be objective and explanatory, not liable to mis-representation and there should be no waste of public money. We will see if this is what actually happens.

Now back reluctantly to the EU. Since the early 1980s the EU has been engaged in a relentless battle for the hearts and minds of hundreds of millions of people on a vast scale, financed from Brussels for one underlying reason.

The long-term project is to convince the populations of the countries in the EU of the merits of ever-closer EU integration and to shift people's loyalties from national to EU institutions leading to the eventual abolition of the nation state.

That they will fail in this eventually and it will all end in tears is certain. Apart from the sheer incompetence of the whole vast set-up, as the famous Russian dissident Vladimir Bukovsky said, communist and socialist bureaucrats never understand human nature, they think they can change it.

Mrs Thatcher, in an introduction to "Statecraft" in 2002 said that "Whatever the flaws of particular nationalisms, national pride and national institutions constitute the best grounding for a functioning democracy".

An instinctive love of country, nationalism before it became a dirty word, is a deeply-felt human instinct. When it is suppressed by force or indoctrination it eventually explodes, perhaps bloodily, as it did in Yugoslavia. We must hope that the EU breaks up before the pressure gets to explosion point. Let us now examine the EU targets for indoctrination and how it works and perhaps you can work out which target area you inhabit.

Europe's youth are a legitimate target in Brussels eyes being regarded as very receptive and the "active population of tomorrow's Europe". They are also seen as especially valuable in that they perform a "messenger service" taking the "right" message to their family and friends maybe even to their elderly suspicious relatives.

To achieve this, the EU has developed a large range of teaching aids and educational modules.

These include pamphlets like "Resources and Contacts", "Let's draw Europe together", "Exploring Europe" and "Euroquest, questions and answers about the EU", all giving the same message that Europe and the EU are the same thing and all completely one-sided. Another is "The path of European Integration" which damns nationalism.

The most outrageous one was called "The Raspberry Ice cream War", with the snappy subtitle "A comic for young people in a peaceful Europe without frontiers". Public outrage in the UK led the government to agree it was ill judged and inaccurate and 75,000 copies destined for UK youth were pulped - an appropriate response to an attempt to throw pixie dust in children's eyes.

For more advanced students there is a teachers' TV programme called "Inside Europe" and the UK government produced a booklet called "Partners in Europe" with the only partly-veiled hint that schools which neglected the European dimension would have this noted in an inspection.

Even study exchanges under an organization called Comenius for schools which have good points carry political associations because of visible EU funding. An organization called Socrates funds educational projects "to promote the development of European citizenship" and is administered in the UK by the Central Bureau for Educational Visits.

To celebrate the then Prime Minister Tony Blair's six-month presidency of the EU (they all got a turn at this), a Partners in Europe pack plus a plastic briefcase was sent to every school. The pack extols the virtues of the EU and says children from nursery age should be taught "European awareness".

This you must realize is the tip of the iceberg, but the pertinent question in the UK is how this deluge of political information to schools is allowed under the 1996 Education Act which forbids the promotion of partisan political views and demands that pupils are offered a balanced presentation of opposing views.

You would have to search long and hard to find any contrary view of the EU anywhere in this huge information output.

For the rest of the population, free information comes from the Prince Programme which produces fact sheets, publications, question and answer booklets and organizes seminars.

Publications with names like "Building the Social Dimension" and "When will the Euro be in Your Pockets?", and "Did you Know" series abound, also historical overviews of the EU, "Europe invests in its Regions" being a good example.

To ensure their distribution the EU has invested in a network of libraries and information centres, many in the UK, including smaller ones for rural areas called Carrefours.

"Relay Europe" tours schools, colleges and universities with interactive videos extolling the EU, giving away calculators and watches with the EU flag on them.

EU-approved speakers are available to address seminars who "must not express any views contrary to those of the Commission". Another part of the overall plan has been the creation and use of "Trojan Horse" organizations which are not quite what they seem on first inspection unless your antennae have been sensitized.

The UK's "Young European Movement" takes the pro-EU message to festivals and conferences and there are the "Young European Federalists", the "Federal Trust" which urges schools to run European citizenship courses and Prom Euro which seeks to allay the fears of the elderly on the euro, even a Europe 2010 Dining Club.

All these artificial front organizations and many more have one thing in common, EU funding.

To influence universities, many hundreds of Jean Monnet academic chairs (you remember him of the killer quote in Chapter Three?), have been financed for projects which must deal specifically with the issue of EU integration. In the last directory of Jean Monnet courses the list of courses in the UK ran to 38 pages. Academics are thus co–opted into EU policy making and are then more likely to support it.

There is even funding for British students to write research papers to promote awareness of European integration.

Then there is the EVS, the European Voluntary Service, where again young people can contribute actively to European integration.

Widespread town twinning seems innocuous enough, but the mayoral oath must make it clear that once again European integration is the primary aim and reason for twinning: "....a successful outcome to this vital venture of peace and prosperity: the EU'. A number of towns and villages have started holding polls to gauge the level of support to un-twin themselves.

Journalists and businessmen are widely offered freebies in the form of lunches and foreign trips and there is lavish entertainment for them at EU summits.

At Maastricht there is a European Journalism Centre which plays a key role in the subversion of the media. It trains journalists from all over the world as well as the EU about European Integration.

An EU spokesman was quoted as saying that about half of all European journalists who wrote stories about his area showed him the full text of any articles for approval before publication. Most journalists in Brussels get their material from the Commission's daily briefing.

Nor is culture neglected. There are European cities of culture, culture months and European youth orchestras and even a Europe Day, the EU's official birthday.

A sad comment on the approach of our own government: it rejected an amendment to the Political Parties, Elections and Referendums Act to ensure government information before a referendum remained factual and impartial on the basis that "neutral material would not work".

An EU document published in French called "An information and communication strategy for the EU" says "Factual information is not sufficient" and calls for pre-emptive targeting of opinion makers, key business people and figures in civil society and women's rights, at a cost, in 2002, of £173 million.

As the Bruges Group quietly says in its Occasional Paper No

45 "The publicity output of the EU not infrequently resembles the communication techniques of both Fascist and Communist regimes". They go on to suggest a number of measures to stop this elimination of free debate such as commitments to objectivity and impartiality which it is unlikely Brussels would understand much less enact.

Next comes the subject of information control which is particularly scary.

Back in 2004, Richard Thomas the Information Commissioner, not an EU commissioner but one of our very own, said that the country might be sleepwalking into a surveillance society. His job is to measure the extent of government snooping on the citizen. He challenges as false and dangerous the regular excuse for restricting freedom that "if you have nothing to hide you have nothing to fear".

While he says that surveillance has its good sides he emphasizes that there are risks and dangers in large-scale systems, that power corrupts and these large-scale infrastructures are liable to large-scale problems.

Also this massive degree of surveillance leads to a general feeling that we are not to be trusted and fosters suspicion.

The study they have done suggests that surveillance will accelerate in years to come and much will be invisible or not obvious to ordinary individuals as they are watched and monitored, and "socially sorted", as the "Surveillance studies network" puts it.

So how much are we watched now?

The UK has over four million CCTV cameras, one-fifth of the world's total and you could be captured on one 300 times a day in London or Edinburgh. This is a crime prevention measure but even a Home Office study decided that the CCTV schemes have had little overall effect on crime levels.

Similarly there has been a huge increase in increasingly sophisticated roadside cameras, generating large sums for the Treasury.

An organization called Privacy International did a national surveillance league table of thirty six countries.

The UK came out as the worst performing western democracy in the category "demonstrating endemic surveillance", along with Russia and China. Germany came top with "significant protection and safeguards". The Commission also did a report on what it imagined Britain would be like in 2016 if present trends continue.

They predict the possibility of total observation of every movement and data base information on everyone. This will be helped by smaller embedded CCTV systems with three-dimensional pictures and universal facial recognition which could even recognize people by the way they walk, plus tracking systems in cars using satellites. In the decade ahead shopping centres will share a huge database which will be fed by data scanners picking up RFID identifiers in clothing tags embedded in customer's clothes. Small children may be mobility tagged.

Another nightmare is the development of radio identification chips which can be implanted in people. By 2016 every movement, purchase and communication could be monitored by a network of interlinked surveillance technologies.

So how far along this road are we?

The government's DNA database merits a look.

The original idea was to record criminals to check and see if they re-offended. It now holds over four million, five hundred thousand samples including those of one and a half million innocent people who may just have been cautioned or cleared and then released and one hundred and fifty thousand children under sixteen including one who threw a slice of cucumber at another and a seven month old girl. It is still increasing rapidly, in 2008 it was disclosed in parliament that 5,000 children are being added every month. At this rate by 2011 some ten million will be on it, some 15 per cent of the population. Even the government admitted in 2007 that there were around half a million mistakes on the base.

It appears to be a classic case of mission creep but if it is the government's intention ultimately to have everyone on it perhaps they should tell us.

A council of EU ministers has recommended that there should be direct automated access between the DNA bases of all EU states.

The other EU states say they only put people on their data bases who are in fact criminals. Ours is fifty times bigger than the French one. Should therefore an innocent British tourist on our data base turn up in a scan at a crime scene abroad he might have a tough time. One potential EU control system which will shortly come into being is the grandly named Galileo. This is the EU version of a global positioning system designed to rival the US and to establish the EU as a space superpower. Among its designed purposes are controlling aerospace, warfare and to run an EU-wide road-charging system which would, besides earning vast sums of money, also conveniently allow the Controllers to know where everyone was at any time. The UK share so far is £500 million.

Even if road charging has gone on the back burner there is however an EU proposal to amend the existing directive on driving licences 91/439/EC to make it mandatory for renewal every ten years.

The excuse is "to complete the free movement of citizens".

This will mean that every ten years, or five if they choose, all the latest security functions can be added to your license. Data added will be limited to road safety data but this can be made to cover nearly anything in EU-speak and will of course be accessed by police and security agencies.

The BBC, or as it is otherwise known, the Brussels Broadcasting Company, is arguably the most powerful opinion-former in the country.

It is worrying therefore that it appears to have a systemic political bias to the left or as someone else put it, institutionalized leftism. The mindset of its 25,000 staff can be summed up as anti-religion, America, Israel, Ulster Unionists, capitalism and anything traditional and that the EU, the UN and multiculturalism are the best things since sliced bread.

From this it follows that anyone who criticizes the EU is xenophobic and probably mad.

I'm aware this sounds a wild and unproven allegation but read on.

The BBC is frequently accused of bias and after one particular investigation the Director General, Mark Thompson admitted that its coverage of European politics had not been impartial and promised to do better. It didn't last.

Back in 2002 three members of the Lords commissioned six surveys of BBC coverage of EU issues from the well-respected Minotaur Media Tracking firm. The main report was some 400 pages plus 600 pages of background analysis plus 780 transcripts going to a further 1,800 pages. This was no casual assessment.

All the reports tell the same story, that the coverage entirely excludes any debate as to whether we should be in the EU at all and the reasons for Euro–scepticism in Britain.

In the report on the general election hardly anyone was interviewed as opposing the EU and even then it was done negatively, and in a series of three half-hour programmes purporting to be on leaving the EU only one person was allowed to put the case for leaving, for 35 seconds.

Newswatch, an independent monitoring company, found in 2007 that it had got worse. During the crucial fourteen weeks prior to the summit at which the constitution was agreed only 2.7 per cent of the available airtime covered the summit and the constitution.

There was also the extraordinary case of the march of 10,000 protesters against the EU through central London some years ago to scenes of considerable enthusiasm. Not one word or picture of it on the BBC, though they did report a demo of a hundred or so in another part of London.

To do your very own survey, assuming the BBC still exists when you get to news-listening age, the key is to listen to the interview techniques. Listen to who gets continually interrupted and who gets a clear run, who gets the dawn slot and who the prime time, the tone of question, sneering or attentive and, if you know anything about the subject, what questions are not asked.

One excuse the BBC gives for lack of coverage on the EU is that none of the main political parties wants to talk about it, for their own reasons.

One final comment on the BBC. The organization BBC Commercial Holdings Limited have accepted a loan of £25million from the EU European Investment Bank which is the EU long-term financing institution and whose stated aim is providing capital investment to further "European integration by promoting EU policies".

The EU-inspired Identity Cards are due to be introduced in due course to fit in with EU passport changes. Your grandfather's generation was always brought up to believe that ID cards and central registers were the tools of dictators and oppression. We are being told that having them or carrying them will not be compulsory for the present. However, citizens will be forced to carry them at all times and produce them on demand otherwise they will be completely useless for their declared purpose of fighting terrorism. Since people coming to this country don't have to have a card for the first three months it makes the terrorism excuse for having them a bit feeble.

The Biometric ID card will be connected to a database called the National Identity Register and the card will be checked on here whenever it is used. It will enable our government and all the various EU databases which they are joined up with to know where you have been and what you are doing at most times, as you will have to produce the card to access banks and government departments and agencies or any other place it is decided.

They admit that this information will be sold on to third parties.

The cards will have a chip storing considerable details of your life, there is no real limit on this and there will be many thousands of people who can access these details. With an EU-wide ID card all this personal information would be available to organizations right across the EU.

It gets worse. Surveillance depends increasingly on radio

frequency identification, RFID chips and transponders and this technology will be able to be built into the new smart ID cards. A fixed transponder will read your position as you walk past it so you can be tracked without even using your card. Should there be any doubt about the EU influence on the government's determination to make the British carry ID cards, the proposed EU constitution states, in Article Three, that "The council may establish measures concerning passports, identity cards......".

The EU Police Chiefs' Task Force agreed that the EU should speed up the universal adoption of ID cards as far back as 2001.

There is also the proposed vast and inevitably leaky NHS database which, although in apparent terminal decline, will store all your medical details. This will be subject to the government's disastrous record on large computer systems using their method of only asking the advice of the people who use it last and too late.

The state has many databases which should be kept separate but the National Identity Register will act as a clearing house for all data collected elsewhere.

Where the EU comes into this is through the Prum Treaty of 2005 which completely evaded the radar of the media. This dealt with "exchange of information on the basis of availability". This is EU speak for stating that any required information on member states' citizens must be given if demanded, meaning access to member states data bases.

Multiple data can now be tabulated and cross referenced, combined with other data to allow for algorithmic surveillance where software works on data and compares it with images on the database.

An ominous system of control which is starting to creep over the horizon is Europol, the EU Police.

As Ashley Mote makes the point in his book "Vigilance", under English Common Law the Rule of Law applies equally to all. All persons are equal and accountable under the Law.

Not quite all though, it seems.

Under Article Eight of the Treaty of Amsterdam members of Europol are "immune from legal process of any kind for acts performed ...... in the exercise of their official functions".

Officially, says Ashley Mote, Europol is required to fight crime, racism and xenophobia. The last two are not definable, being attitudes, so this is a form of mind control, clamping down on free speech and expression of opinion.

Also European Extradition Measures which came into force in 2004 could cause people in this country to be extradited to a country in Europe accused of things which are not crimes in this country; this on the demand of any magistrate in any EU state without presenting any evidence.

Already they have substantial files on British subjects, who may not even have committed crimes. Writing this book may well qualify your grandfather! I say this because Europol's database covering all EU states has at least 56 fields of data on each individual including of course political views. These are not available to the British police but it has the right to ask British police to investigate British nationals. The potential use of these powers in the wrong hands is chilling and who controls Europol is unclear.

The granting of diplomatic immunity to the police is more dangerous than you can imagine. It was never debated in Parliament but pushed through by statutory instrument. Even the notorious Russian secret police, the KGB, didn't have diplomatic immunity.

Behind Europol is the EGF, the EU Gendarmerie. Italy, Spain, France, Holland and Portugal have volunteered to form this force whose remit is "the restoration of public order" and again over which there is no scrutiny or accountability. These EU states agreed in 2000 to "provide up to 5,000 officers for international missions across the range of conflict prevention and crisis management operations". Also, " the maintenance of public order in the event of disturbances".

This force was put on an official footing at the signing of a Treaty at Velsa in Holland on 18th October, 2007.

Although not having a militarised police force we are not entitled to take part, under Article 6.3 of the Treaty, we can join by "agreement".

Mr Miliband, our Foreign Secretary at the time refused, in answer to MPs questions, to give an assurance that this force would not be invited into the UK. They can enter by government consent, though once inside they could only be removed by order from Brussels, as the supreme authority.

The record of European armed gendarmerie in Spain and France is not comforting. Does a peaceful protest march rate as a "disturbance"? There has always been a right to peaceful protest but it is being subtly eroded. A stand at the Suffolk agricultural show was having a famous time selling T-shirts printed "Bollocks to Blair" which was vulgar but hardly warranted the police closing in and cautioning wearers. When the news got around they sold out. Then there was the lady arrested for reading out the names of the war dead in Iraq at the Cenotaph. This was under the auspices of the Serious and Organized Crime and Police Act of 2005.

Perhaps another cause for concern was an order from the Home Office, as it was then, for our police in 1998. This was for 30,000 sub machine guns, 100,000 rounds of ammunition, 8 sniper rifles and 12,000 12-bore riot-control shotguns, which were delivered to the army base at Catterick.

Makes you wonder if the EGF and our government are planning ahead in case they have to subdue an insurrection of irritated pensioners?

Both the EU and our government have used what they have termed "benevolent crises" to justify further encroachment on liberties. Even before 9/11 a senior EU official was lamenting the lack of such a crisis, and the war on terror is a continual handy excuse.

The Olympics in 2012 appear a wonderful reason for a whole swathe of new police powers.

A government memo asks "To what extent should the expectation of liberty be eroded by legitimate intrusions in the interests of security of the wider public". It goes on to say "Increasing (public) support could be possible through the piloting of certain approaches in high profile ways such as the London Olympics".

Another freedom which has been quietly cancelled is the once-held belief that an Englishman's home was his castle.

In 2007 it was established by the Centre for Policy Studies that state officials have 266 justifications to enter your home. In most cases entry, if denied, can be gained by force and obstruction can result in fines or criminal charges. Some of these rights of entry come from EU directives, the rest from acts of Parliament.

The latest intrusion into privacy and loss of freedom is a new law compelling phone companies to retain and make available all land line and mobile telephone calls.

The phrase "Big brother is watching over you" has now come true.

A Statutory instrument implementing, the EU Data Retention Directive now empowers our government to bug phone lines, open our e-mail and access mail, enabling it to discover our calling patterns, e-mail usage, where we have been and our network of friends and colleagues.

Further over 600 public bodies and quangos as well as the security services and the police can now request covert access to the records of the entire population for every imaginable reason, "economic well-being, public safety, even minor offences, such as dropping litter or parking. The much heralded "Data Protection Act" can be completely ignored by the catch all claim of being "in the public interest".

There is an Information Commissioner, charged with oversite of the Act, but he is in effect powerlesss due to Whitehall embedded limitations in his powers.

There is no record available of what the information would be used for and no public accountability.

Lots of verbal assurances about safeguards of course.

If you have not yet read George Orwell's book "1984" then please borrow it from your parents. It used to be seen as frightening fiction of a horrific future dictatorship with complete surveillance and control of everyone. Look for the parallels, they may be more apparent to you. Another scary novel painting a picture of future lost freedom is "The Aachen Memorandum" by the historian Andrew Roberts who was at

Cambridge with your mother. This deals with a Britain still in the EU in around 2045. One hopes it will stay fiction. If you have got this far you will begin to realize, looking back, how stealthily our freedom was taken from us.

As James Madison elegantly said long ago, "There are more instances of the abridgement of the freedom of the people by gradual and silent encroachments of those in power than by violent and sudden usurpation".

6

Where it all goes wrong

This chapter is an attempt to illustrate the basic fault lines in the whole EU concept and to spell out some of the schemes going wrong in this year of grace 2008. In ten years time there may be more and worse but some of this lot may have collapsed in tears.

This is because one concept that our EU masters have never taken on board is the wisdom of the ancient advice that when you are in a hole – stop digging.

There is no shortage of examples of gigantic foul-ups but the causes are often highly complex and it is a hard job presenting them in a form which does not make even the attentive reader's eyes glaze over and induce a strong wish to be doing something else.

Perhaps the biggest problem is the enormous scale of endemic corruption. Corruption in a country usually starts at the bottom of the social pile and corrupts its way up.

By contrast, and very similar to the old Soviet communist model, corruption in the EU starts at the top and spreads downwards.

This is made childishly simple by the EU accounting system, or lack of it. The official auditors' court have to, their credit, refused to pass the accounts for thirteen years in succession. The Commission has got over this little local difficulty by ignoring the auditors.

To explain the scale of the problem, many hundreds of on-going enquiries into fraud by EU officials going back many years are still unresolved.

In 2007, the Commission itself reported that 1,155 million Euros disappeared through "irregularities" in 2006 though this, they said, did include mistakes made in good faith. They also admitted that 320 million euros had been deliberately stolen, nearly one million a day.

The EU anti-corruption commissar for 2007, one Siim Kallas, was embroiled in a major financial scandal in the 1990s when he was governor of the central bank of Estonia.

In 1999 the President of the Commission and twenty two commissioners were forced to resign over fraud and mismanagement. Some were quickly re-appointed including a failed British politician Neil Kinnock. He was then appointed to combat fraud and eradicate corruption.

After three years he admitted that no official had been dismissed.

Also he seems to have misunderstood his brief.

A lady called Marta Andreason, a senior Spanish accountant, had been appointed to clean up the Commission's accounts. She found, as Christopher Booker says in his book "The Great Deception," serious and glaring shortcomings, a complete lack of double-entry book-keeping and a computer system wide open to alteration and fraud.

After reporting this to Mr Kinnock and the Commissioners and getting no response she put her case to the European Parliament in a letter. She was very quickly sacked by Kinnock and her name and character blackened by the EU spin machine. Mr Kinnock, the Commission Vice President, tried to silence her and she claims she was followed by unknown men and her e-mails hacked into.

Another example is that of Douglas Watt of the Court of Auditors, who lodged a complaint about corruption and nepotism within the actual court of Auditors. He was summarily sacked.

In 2004 Hans-Martin Tillack, a German journalist working for *Stern* Magazine, was arrested in the middle of the night and all his computer records and notebooks impounded. The arresting officers were from OLAF, the EU fraud investigation unit. Mr Tillack had been investigating the disappearance of millions of pounds from the EU Humanitarian Aid Office.

This program to which as long ago as 2000 the UK was

contributing £700 million a year was described by the UK minister for overseas aid as "the worst development agency in the world".

Several other whistleblowers of various nationalities have been victimized and eventually sacked. One MEP deplored that the culture of Brussels did more to cover wrong-doing than unveil problems.

The line peddled by EU apologists is that the member states bear the responsibility. However the funds paid into the EU treasury by member states are controlled exclusively by the Commission as designed in the treaty.

As a contrast to fraud and corruption, hundreds of millions of pounds, up to 15 per cent of the budget is underspent and just sits there, which looks like honest incompetence.

On the other side, to make corruption a little easier, officials working for a huge range of EU institutions have been given diplomatic immunity from prosecution. Unbelievable though it sounds, this immunity is also conferred on "the members of their families who form part of their household".

Ashley Mote in his book "Vigilance" sums up the feelings of the Auditors on EU accounts.

They criticized "inconsistent and inadequate day-to-day accounting records, tardy and incomplete documents, haphazard and wildly inaccurate estimating, vast sums disappearing without trace, assets and liabilities understated, hopelessly inadequate credit and cash control, regular payments made without regard for need or purpose, commitments made to spend non existent funds, money paid to intermediaries that subsequently took years to reach the intended beneficiary, and, if all that was not more than enough, the total lack of a unified accounting system across all directorates and institutions".

There is in fact an EU Parliamentary committee on budget control but they report that they are unable to get any facts due to obstruction and misleading information from other departments. Furthermore, neither the European Central Bank nor the European Investment Bank will open their records to fraud investigators.

A senior corporate lawyer, having worked for years for the EU, commented on endemic corruption and making laws "on the hoof". He described the situation as "beyond redemption".

In Britain anger at this state of affairs has turned over the years to contempt, for they know that Brussels will never change and in truth people no longer much care. It is similar to the state of a marriage when it is finally over.

The Common Fisheries Policy

This is enforced on the lunatic basis that any fish caught and hauled on board which doesn't fit into a strictly allocated quota must be thrown back dead into the sea.

Several million tons of perfectly edible dead fish pollute the bottom of the North sea alone every year.

This madness all began in 1972 when the then Prime Minister, Edward Heath, frantic to get his brainwashed country into the then EEC, threw in the offer of British fishing waters as a "common resource".

This was much to the gratified astonishment of the much cleverer people he was negotiating with. He did this on the often quoted basis that the fishermen were electorally insignificant and expendable.

The Norwegians who owned the other half of the North Sea were offered considerable concessions in 1972 to join and give up their fishing grounds, but their fisheries minister resigned and their fortunate country rejected the EEC in a referendum. Their fishing grounds are still in good heart, while what is now the EU area is heading for an ecological disaster.

British fishermen were at first allowed to catch fish on the basis of the EU phrase "relative stability", that is in proportion to what they had traditionally caught.

This was until Spain joined the EU and room had to be found for her vast fleet of trawlers. A new EU phrase was now coined, "equal access". The new carve-up was on the basis of the size of fishing fleets.

Since Spain had a large economic dependence on fishing her huge fleet was to be allowed the great majority of the catch.

However this was put off until 2002 and, to keep the Spanish and Portuguese happy meanwhile, the EU bought up fishing rights down the West African coast until they would be allowed access to the North Sea and Irish Sea.

Naturally this destroyed the local fishing industries and industrial fishing devastated large areas of delicate eco-system.

In parallel back in the North Sea the British and Scandinavian fleets were scaled down in a series of cuts disguised as conservation measures as the Spanish fleet was expanded and modernized with EU grants. At this time Spain was getting 52 per cent of all fishing subsidies.

Also the British fleet has always been zealously over regulated with fines of £50,000 for one box of fish landed over quota at a regulation cost every year of 20 per cent of the total worth of the industry. This compares with the Spanish inspectors who are reputed to mostly stay in Madrid.

In 2002 there were serious proposals to reform the whole system with a start to general fleet reductions, to stop subsidies for new and bigger trawlers, institute re-training grants and most importantly to have teams of inspectors visiting fishing ports.

However the French and Spanish soon put a stop to that. After a long telephone chat between the Spanish President and Romano Prodi, the President of the EU Commission, the Danish Director General of Fishing Policies was sacked on the order of Mr. Prodi and that was the end of any talk of reform.

Over the years thousands of British and Irish fishing boats have been burnt on the beach, for if they give up the struggle their boats, by EU decree, must be destroyed.

The Common Fisheries Policy was meant to preserve and maintain fish stocks. It has resulted in the virtual destruction of the British fishing industry and a pending ecological disaster.

Whatever the EU say it is trying to do, the result seems to achieve the exact opposite.

The Common Agricultural Policy

Having dealt with the ruin of the British fishing industry, it seems appropriate to deal next with the Byzantine EU system of control of farming.

The primary purpose of the Common Agricultural Policy (CAP), was to protect French farmers.

The UK was deliberately excluded from joining the then EEC by the French under De Gaulle who vetoed our application to join until the rules of the CAP were stitched up tight.

It was organized so that it was financed by levies on imported goods as the main source of income. This hardly affected France at all but had a severe effect on the UK as she imported the bulk of her supplies from the Commonwealth. As we abandoned trade with the Commonwealth, France took over. That is an over simplification of a long period of devious deals but an accurate summary.

As with most EU schemes the method of farm subsidy was complicated. They were on two levels, direct payments to farmers and "discretionary funds". These last had to be matched by an equivalent sum from the member state but following an agreement at Fontainbleau, the UK treasury found itself paying most of these funds and so decided not to match them which also suited the government politically. Thus British farmers have to compete with other EU farmers enjoying a much higher level of funding. There is an EU report which lists all the national systems of funding. The UK has the shortest list, "none".

A report stated that British farmers' incomes had dropped by 50 per cent in one year. In the rest of the EU farmers' incomes increased by 14 per cent in the five years up to 2000.

One result of the CAP was the production of enormous mountains of beef, butter and grain surplus. These were sold at a loss to the Russians or dumped on third world economies causing great distress to their agricultural economies.

In 2006 the system was reformed though altered would be more accurate. To try and stop the formation of wine lakes and beef and grain mountains farmers would now qualify for subsidies just by "keeping their land in agricultural condition". Needless to say everyone with a paddock for a pony started to claim subsidy and the Rural Payments Agency collapsed under a mountain of applications. Real farmers' payments were delayed for a year or more to the dismay of their overdrafts, some went bankrupt and the EU, to rub salt in it, fined the UK millions for the delay.

The new system doesn't appear to be achieving its purpose on the Continent either. In 2006 nearly a billion bottles of French and Italian plonk were bought up by the EU to turn into industrial alcohol.

If you mention Foot and Mouth to farmers around you they will probably stop smiling.

In 1991 and 1993 EU contingency plans were drawn up against the possibility of a foot and mouth outbreak in Europe, for the EU had exercised ultimate control over Foot and Mouth policy since the 1980s.

A disastrous outbreak hit the UK in 2001 resulting in the slaughter of nearly eleven million animals, a high proportion not infected and the animals being either buried in vast pits or burnt on giant funeral pyres. It crippled British farming and the tourist industry for years. The financial cost was some nine billion pounds.

Unfortunately the EU and the UK were so hopelessly unprepared for the scale of the outbreak that the obvious policy of vaccination was not remotely possible. In 2002 a new directive stated that any future epidemic would be controlled by vaccination under EU direction. This directive has been kept secret ever since.

A new limited outbreak in 2007 was still controlled by the same slaughter system used in 2001.

Now a bit on abattoirs, and the need for local ones to prevent the stress on animals taken on long journeys.

In the 1990s the EU decreed that all abattoirs had to be supervised by a vet. On the Continent vets are employed to do the job done here by highly trained meat inspectors. The enormous extra cost caused about half of British slaughterhouses to close including most of the invaluable small local ones thus causing animals to endure much longer and stressful journeys.

It was suggested that these vets, a majority imported from Spain, should be paid only for hours worked, but Brussels said they must be paid full-time even when there was no work, so the closures continued. Some of the foreign vets employed had only had two weeks training in meat inspection.

Farming is hard work and can be stressful. When you add on the mind-numbing amount of paperwork thrown at them by officials it makes you wonder why they bother.

As Ross Clark explains in his engaging book "How to label a Goat" just the claims process to get the subsidy goes like this:

First you ring up the Rural Payments Agency and ask for the 24 page SP5a application form.

You then have to read the 112-page Single Payments Scheme Handbook and Guidance, plus six other documents.

Having completed the form and sent it off, you must apply for a holding number for your land. This involves filling in another fifteen page form with 40 pages of guidance.

You then wait forever for your money, hoping the bank will be as patient.

A CAP rule for the experienced farmer to keep the land in good condition is that if there is a puddle on the field beyond twenty meters from the gate, he is not allowed to plough. This is the level of infantile orders given to farmers who possibly know their own land better than some remote bureaucrat in a warm office.

Defence

Whether we are at war or not the main function of any government is to defend the country.

To fulfill this our armed forces have to be kept properly equipped and manned.

Since 1998 when our then Prime Minister signed up to the idea of a European Defence Force at St. Malo the government and our Ministry of Defence have been besotted with FRES. This is the "Future Rapid Effect System" which, as Christopher Booker has pointed out, is a cut-price version of the "Future Combat System" being developed by the U.S. Army.

Thousands of vehicles with a total lifetime cost of approaching £100 billion were ordered from EU firms in spite of cheaper and better ones available from a US and British consortia to bolster up a "European Defence Identity".

All these expensive vehicles are designed to be satellite-controlled by the EU Galileo satellite system. This was set up in 2000 to match the astonishingly successful US Global Positioning System, GPS.

China joined in with Galileo to begin with but has now left and gone off with the know how.

Eight large companies were involved in the project in 2007, but were worried that it wouldn't be profitable and pulled out. The whole project is six years behind schedule and only a trial satellite is yet in orbit of the thirty one planned. The other slight problem with Galileo for the British army is that it would stop us working alongside American forces, our traditional and strongest allies, as their satellites would identify any forces not in their system as potential enemies. The surreal progress of this vast project, was described by the forthright MP Gwyneth Dunwoody, as "not one pig flying in orbit, this is a herd of pigs with golden trotters, platinum tails and diamond eyes". Britain alone will have to now pay around 1.7 billion pounds for our 17 per cent of the project, and once the new constitution is ratified the Commission will have control over EU space policy and can just charge the cost to its yearly budget.

The US system by the way is free while the EU one is planned to haul in huge profits.

The other services are in a similar muddle, expensive new destroyers were equipped with French anti-aircraft missiles inferior to the US model and lacking anti-submarine weapons, weaponry useful to an island which cannot feed itself and was nearly defeated in two world wars by submarines.

On the same theme and I admit I'm prejudiced, the first Queen Elizabeth said that "it is upon the Navy, under the good providence of God, that the wealth, strength and safety of the kingdom do chiefly depend". The government acting on this good advice, (and I admit I can't pin it on the EU), a complete class of destroyers has been moth-balled, and there are warnings that half the remainder of the Royal Navy will have to go due to lack of money.

The RAF is lumbered with the Eurofighter designed to fight the Russians n the 1980s and costing some £20 billion each but not ideal for the wars we are fighting in this century.

On the subject of the planned "EU Defence Identity", an interesting phrase used by the British armed forces is "multi-national troop degradation syndrome". This concerns the tendency of a multi-national force to debase to the level of the least efficient group.

A glimmer of common sense has broken through to the Ministry of Defence following outrage at the deaths of troops in the Middle East due to inferior equipment. The MOD has delayed buying equipment for EU fantasy wars and suddenly in 2007 the army was getting a limited quantity of high quality US based equipment.

The Railways

The railways were privatized in the 1990s and it would seem obvious that each company should be responsible for the tracks its trains ran on. The reason this did not happen and the reason for the years of complete shambles since was the EU directive 91/440 EEC which decreed that the train operators and the infrastructure should be separated. The EU reason for this was to encourage train companies to operate across national frontiers while allowing each nation to control its own tracks. This was inflicted on us even though we are the one country in the EU with no cross-border railways except for Eurostar.

This illogical and impracticable system allows everyone to blame the others for problems.

Two further directives, 2991/13/EC and 2991/14/EC2 are now adding further confusion to freight services, allowing rail companies to buy up "train paths" across national boundaries.

Health and Pensions

By the time you are earning a reasonable salary the cost of providing pensions especially to those on the government payroll will take a sizeable chunk of it. That's just in this country. In Continental Europe it could be catastrophic. If by then we have joined the euro we will be sharing the cost of European pensions. Way back in 1997 the EU pensions liability was twelve hundred billion pounds. A US National Intelligence report said at worst it could lead to the disintegration of the euro.

The National Health Service

It would seem difficult to further complicate the workings of the NHS but the European Working Time Directive has had a stab at it.

This Directive has the effect of limiting the time junior doctors can work to 58 hours per week which is laudable in theory, as tired doctors can make fatal mistakes. My daughter didn't make any, but twenty years ago she was regularly putting in over one hundred hours a week.

This Directive resulted in a drastic lack of junior doctors, and to make things worse the European Court of Justice then ruled that rest and sleeping breaks must be included in the 58 hours. It also had an adverse effect on the training of junior doctors, in that they were no longer exposed to enough variety and number of disorders to attain competence in their management especially during evenings and at weekends. In doctor-speak this will "decrease learning opportunities and clinical experience".

Another consequence of the Working Time Directive was that it made sense to centralize services resulting in closure of accident and emergency centres and patients often having then to travel large distances.

The effects are not for a change entirely the fault of the EU as the government had six years to prepare for this problem waiting to happen and did nothing.

One quality newspaper succinctly described the directive as typical of European legislation, "Utopian in aspiration, poorly conceived in practice".

Metrication

In 2000 EU regulations were introduced to make it illegal to use traditional measures like pounds, pints and inches. This was done without bothering to repeal an act of parliament that said the traditional measures were legal and it was pushed through in spite of widespread opposition.

The Metric Martyrs, a brave bunch of market stall holders, with legal backing took their case to court and for the first time the courts ruled out loud that EU law took precedence over British law.

Compulsory metrication as well as causing great confusion and costing many fortunes was enforced ruthlessly, many were prosecuted, imperial scales were destroyed and traders had to buy new ones.

The roads were left for a while with miles and yards but the long term plan is that kilometres will be forced on us. In 2007 the Brussels Commission said it would no longer impose metrication on Britain; nevertheless, the British Government is still prosecuting market traders for selling vegatables in pounds (see Chaper Seven).

Metrication was forced on Europe by Napoleon, again ruthlessly enforced and based, it now transpires, on false mathematics. The traditional measures are based on human measures like the length of a foot and originated, the British Weights and Measures Society claims, in pre–history. Our traditional system is still used in most of the rest of the world and the EU has relaxed its rulings a little since it found it was harming trade with the US.

Canada went metric but the old-accepted measures are creeping back so perhaps there is still hope for freedom of choice.

Waste Disposal

Not an exciting subject but a classic example of EU legislation having the opposite effect to that intended.

On the one hand the EU classified more and more substances as "hazardous waste", from old vehicles to empty paint tins to any electrical equipment, amounting to a huge tonnage going up by a large percentage every year.

An example of this was the End of Life Vehicle Directive 2000/53. This requires the sorting out of all the components of scrapped cars into various classifications, which is so costly that many scrapyards are just giving up.

The entirely predictable result is an epidemic of fly tipping and burnt out abandoned cars.

On the other hand the EU reduced the number of landfill sites in the UK licensed to take hazardous waste from 218 to 10.

Also the waste incineration directive allows only the destruction of waste by incineration but says nothing on burning it for energy recovery.

This has stopped the recovery of waste oil for treatment for re-use or burning for energy and even threatened a £65million scheme in Scotland to turn sewage sludge into pellets for fuel for a power station.

Health Products

Some 5,000 health food products are threatened with being banned by the EU Food Supplements Directive. This allows vitamins and minerals, even quite simple ones, only to be used if they are on an approved list.

To get on this list by 2009 involves huge cost and sophisticated testing which will rule out most small firms and leave the field wide open to multi-national companies. The EU Advocate General concluded the directive was invalid but the European Court of Justice over-ruled him.

By 2009 a wide variety of health food products will simply vanish from the shelves.

Value Added Tax

Value added tax, VAT, is a Euro tax and was a hidden condition of our joining the EEC in 1973. The EU aim is a single "harmonized" VAT regime as a first step to a unified EU tax system.

The government is forbidden to reduce to zero any VAT rate on any item once it has been established. The control of VAT money is planned to be centralized eventually in Brussels then re-distributed as they decide.

The UK's zero tax rate on a number of items is planned eventually to be abolished which will raise many more billions in tax but which will fall heaviest on poorer people.

At present in 2008 VAT is zero-rated in the UK on:

Food in shops.
Children's clothes.
Books and newspapers.
Public transport.
New houses.
Water and sewage services.
Pharmaceuticals.

In ten years time many of them will no doubt have become VAT-able.

The Euro

European Monetary Union resulting in the adoption of the Euro was designed by the European political elite as an instrument for achieving full economic and political union. A handy side effect would be the gutting of national parliaments.

The benefits it was supposed to bring were intense competition, leaping productivity, higher growth and rising living standards. These somehow failed to appear.

The EMU entails one European Central Bank, one set of rules on budget deficits which the larger countries ignore when it suits them, a single rate of interest and a central monetary policy.

What has resulted is a sprawling government structure, dubious political ambitions, a collection of governments liable to quarrel and a superbank with secret policies.

The one-size-fits-all interest rate puts severe strain on Europe's southern tier states, especially Italy whose economy has on occasion gone into reverse with huge public debt.

The usual Italian answer to looming economic disaster is to devalue the currency but having joined the Euro this is no longer an option.

The UK government was all set to bounce the country into the Euro spending millions on preparatory work and propaganda before asking the people in a promised referendum. Fortunately the idea fell out of favour with the then Chancellor of the Exchequer Gordon Brown, and it would seem now politically very difficult, though not for the right reasons.

This was fortunate because even the government estimated the cost of the changeover at the time as £36 billion.

The cost was not limited in Europe just to the setting-up costs. The levelling up of prices while people were trying to adjust to the new currency pushed up the cost of living considerably.

An extraordinarily large number of people, according to opinion polls, would dearly like their old currencies back but until it all collapses in tears this is unlikely. Keep an interested eye on Italy.

Christina Speight, a doughty opponent of the EU, quotes the views of some of the European elite on the introduction of the single currency.

In France, Raymond Barre, a former French Prime Minister: "I have never understood why public opinion about European matters should be taken into account".

In Spain, Felipe Gonzales, another former Prime Minister. "The single currency is the greatest abandonment of sovereignty since the foundation of the European Community".

In Germany, Hans Tietmeyer, then president of the Bundesbank, "Monetary Union is a path of no return".

Long ago, Mayer Rothschild, "Give me control of a nation's currency and I care not who makes the laws".

And in Britain? Mr Hoon, the then British Defence Minister, "The Euro raises no constitutional issues at all".

7

What we have already lost

It is very difficult to assess what we have lost in the way of freedoms, because anything we have signed up to or any of the opt outs gained in the various treaties can be overturned or re-interpreted. Anything in any treaty can be overturned by use of the catch all Clause Four in Article Six of the Amsterdam treaty.

This states that "The union shall provide itself with the means necessary to attain its objectives and carry through its policies". This is a declaration that the EU can do whatever it wants to attain its purpose of an integrated federal state.

One would think though that there would be a simple way to list the freedoms we have lost. All one needs to do surely is to go through the various treaties our politicians have signed in our name.

To illustrate that it isn't that simple, John Major, Prime Minister in the 1990s, came home after signing one treaty, Maastricht, and asked his civil servants to go through the treaty and find out exactly what he had signed us up to.

The EU does not do simple and straightforward. Everything in a treaty must have different possibilities of interpretation from its deliberately ambivalent phrasing. Any decision can then be decided the "correct" way by the European Court of Justice.

One of the main haemorrhages of freedom in all these treaties has been the seemingly innocuous transfer of powers to qualified majority voting (QMV).

When this happens we can be outvoted on the policy, however vital it may be to us, as we no longer have a veto.

We have never used our veto on anything, our politicians

being too scared of being made to go and sit on the naughty step, but it was useful in reserve.

So what have we lost? The Treaty of Rome set up the European Commission and established that the Commission alone could initiate legislation. This treaty established the European Economic Community and European citizenship, plus provisions on Foreign and Security policies and in Justice and Home affairs.

Here the foundations of a European federal state and political union were laid. At Maastricht the Committee of the Regions was formed from the 111 regions of the Community. They were given powers to be "consulted" on legislation.

The Treaty of Rome was amended to provide for monetary union and the EU was created.

As I said all Europeans were promoted to be European citizens even if they didn't ask for it.

Maastricht also established "competences" or control over consumer protection, public health, education and culture among other things. QMV appeared, being extended in voting in the Council of Ministers.

At the Treaty of Amsterdam QMV was spread to a further twelve areas including statistics, which is useful if you want to prove the EU is doing well.

A High Representative for Foreign and Security policy was created, in fact an embryo EU foreign minister.

It extended co–decision which could mean whatever you wanted it to mean.

In 2001 at the treaty of Nice, QMV was again extended over thirty nine more areas, including visas, asylum and immigration. We could no longer decide who should be allowed into the country.

This reduced the voting influence of Britain in the Council of Ministers to 8.4 per cent.

Eurojust was established, a title straight out of Orwell's 1984.

There were pages of tedious sounding clauses which could be carefully tucked away until needed, a flexibility clause of the Amsterdam Treaty was extended, the suspension provision amended, new provisions for implementing the Common European Security and Defence Policy, which was the beginning of the EU army.

There is admittedly no point in listing the freedoms we have given away in the hope they can be regained by argument or diplomacy, for as long as we stay members of the EU they can never be regained.

This is because of what is known as the "*acquis communitaire*" where any power surrendered to the EU by national governments can never be given back. There can be no negotiation.

So what else have we lost?

Firstly there are the small familiar things of everyday life which give "feel" to a country. A lot of these result from the Directive on compulsory metrication imposed with complete ruthlessness on a resentful and largely unwilling population.

As detailed in the previous chapter it led to the formation of the "Metric Martyrs", a widespread group of tradespeople, butchers, grocers and stallholders who with bravery and determination stood up to persecution by local authorities They had great public support.

Stallholders were even threatened with prosecution for shouting out "twenty pence a pound" instead of kilos, such was the government's determination to suppress any resistance to the directive.

We also lost our yards and inches, acres gave way to hectares, pints changed to litres. The familiar changed to the awkward and foreign. They did graciously permit us to keep our miles on the roads, the cost of changeover being probably too prohibitive. The BBC went into full metric mode immediately even talking about metric measures in countries which were still using imperial.

Extraordinarily, however, in June 2007 the Commission changed its mind and ruled to allow indefinitely the use of imperial measures alongside metric ones and unbelievably "the statement of intent to allow traders to use imperial who wish to do so'.

This change of heart may have had something to do with

expensive trade difficulties with the US, if metric was made completely compulsory and if the imperial system used in the USA was banned in exports. Unfortunately most traders have had to expensively re-equip with metric scales.

These are examples of the familiar personal things which have been lost and which give "feel" to everyday life even though apparently superficial.

Far more important are where thousands of jobs and livelihoods and a way of life have been destroyed.

Fishermen and farmers are by nature of their jobs independent-minded and tough, dealing daily with the elements and it has been quite an achievement to reduce them to the level of supplicants and form fillers for Brussels.

Our legal system is also controlled by EU law as to a large extent is the actual making of law.

The criminal justice system and the police are semi-independent but the EU is steadily encroaching on them too.

The currency is still intact apart from going metric and more or less under our control since we edged away from joining the Euro.

The ancient and effective system of local government, of parish, district and county councils is effectively under the control of the powerful unelected Regional Assemblies. These are due to be "abolished" in 2009 but replaced by Regional Development Authorities, RDAs, originally set up in 1999 but with all the same powers, still taking their direction from Brussels and without even the pretence of being elected.

Business is increasingly controlled and stifled by red tape. The cost of over-control in the EU as a whole has been estimated by Brussels as a percentage of total EU Gross Domestic Product. Putting the same percentage on our GDP, this amounts to some £20 billions per year. However, the multiplicity of indirect costs, like trying to run a small business if you are not fluent in bureaucratic language, could multiply this several times.

The nearest estimate of costs to the UK and it can only be an estimate, is the nice round figure of £50 billion per year but it could be double that. Think for instance of the huge cost of the army of officials and inspectors and their inflated salaries and pensions.

Foreign policy is affected all ways but it can best be summed up by the story of the tourist in Whitehall who asks a policeman which side the Foreign Office was on. The policeman's response was "That's a very good question, sir".

Education appears to be our concern but a tendency of the EU to re-write history does not augur well.

Similarly our tax policies appear to be our concern but there is much EU talk about an "integrated tax policy".

Defence and the armed services are gradually slipping out of our control though this does not appear on the surface. Ancient regiments in the army are being combined into "super regiments" to match the organization of the proposed EU army with all the loss of hundreds of years of tradition which make up the spirit of an army. When the Royal Navy starts flying the EU stars instead of the White Ensign then it will be time to start worrying.

Perhaps the best answer to what we have lost is found in the answer given by Baroness Amos, Minister of State to the Foreign Office, in 2002. She was asked the number of regulations enacted and which we are now subject to from EU legislation. Her answer was that "as far as the government has been enabled to verify the number was 101,811". She didn't sound very sure.

Nor does this include the huge raft of legislation we took on when we joined the then EEC back in the seventies but "it would be too expensive to try and estimate that number" says the government.

The authoritative publication *eurofacts* states the number of regulations the British are subject to as a result of EU membership is not known but it is probably now in excess of 200,000. There goes freedom.

8

Where freedom is vanishing

Think of me ten years ago trying to describe and come to conclusions on a frighteningly-fast ongoing process of takeover. We are now, in the next year or so, coming to the crunch point and the potentially final loss of your freedom.

Someone sagely said that freedom is like being pregnant, you are or you are not, there is no half-way house.

The most deadly threat to Britons as free persons in a free country is the proposed EU Constitution under the guise of a new EU Lisbon Treaty, to replace the Constitution rejected in 2006 in a national referendum by the French and Dutch. The British weren't allowed to have one.

So bear with me and I will tell you in as few words as possible where this threat came from.

This has been researched in detail in the book called "The Great Deception" by Booker and North. If you find copies are banned or just unobtainable in ten years' time then you will know that they wrote in vain.

The first person we have to thank is an Italian communist, Altiero Spinelli who in his prison cell during the war had a vision of a United States of Europe, to be assembled over a long period without openly revealing the end purpose. The peoples of Europe, he planned, should not be consulted until a "constituent assembly" was ready to draw up a "constitution'. This was in 1941!

The next two originators were Arthur Salter, an English civil servant and Jean Monnet, a French brandy salesman.

Their idea of a United States of Europe was a new form of supra-national government run by technocrats beyond the control of elected governments, elected politicians and certainly electorates. They too realized they could never succeed if their true purpose became evident.

The final originator was Paul-Henri Spaak, a Prime Minister of Belgium who thought up a brilliant way to disguise the political purpose of the project. This was by disguising the project as only being concerned with economic matters and cooperation, hence the original "Common Market" under which deceit we joined.

In 2003 it was decided the time was ripe to abandon subterfuge and wrap up the takeover in the form of a European Constitution.

Brought forward before nine new countries were admitted, some having just escaped from communism, it was to set the whole thing in concrete. It was advertised and promoted as a document to bring the EU and the people closer together and in the UK as a mere tidying-up exercise of loose ends of previous treaties.

One hundred and five carefully selected delegates from fifteen countries met under the chairmanship of former French President Valéry Giscard d'Estaing to formulate it. An impression of public consultation was created by consulting non-governmental organizations, NGOs in Brussels speak. These NGOs were almost all funded by the EU, and no organization which was in any way even slightly critical was included.

Two British delegates, the labour MP Gisela Stuart and the Conservative MP David Heathcote-Amory, thoroughly alarmed, proposed a number of amendments and mildly sceptic reservations which were totally ignored. The result, after many months, was a document running to three hundred and fifty pages incorporating all the previous treaties.

Its form as usual was deliberately ambiguous, spattered with contradictory objectives such as "united in diversity".

The vagueness enabled many vital issues left to be finally decided by the European Court of Justice, whose guiding purpose in all judgments is held to be "ever-closer union".

In effect it was a vast blank cheque where its full implications would only be realized when it was ratified and agreed by national governments.

Someone summed it up as the ramblings of a slightly pompous megalomaniac. The British Institute of Directors gave the more sober opinion that the additional powers written into the document were "effectively limitless".

In a misguided attempt to con the public our government offered to send a complete copy of the constitution to anyone who asked and your aged grandfather has one on the shelf as I write. I have attempted to read it too, unlike most of the politicians who voted for it. Believe me I have dealt with it gently.

The first attempt at a draft constitution was published in October 2002 and discussed at the Dublin conference in June 2004. It specified a flag, the anthem, the motto Unity in Diversity, the euro currency and, let joy be unconfined, Europe Day on 9th of May. April 1st was rejected for some reason. A good day, 9th of May my fellow churchwarden suggests, to fly the flag of St. George.

The new powers taken were divided into "Exclusive competences" where the EU had total control and "Shared competences" where member states kept power if the EU didn't want it. The result is much the same.

Referendums were started in the countries which had either decided to have one thinking the result would be yes, where political pressure forced it on a government as in the UK or where their own constitution insisted on it.

The mind-set of the EU to referenda and its attitude to democracy are summed up by Louis Michel, once a Belgian Foreign Minister, commenting at the time of the Nice Treaty which Ireland initially rejected: "I personally think that it is very dangerous to organize referendums when you're not sure to win them. If you lose the referendum it's a big problem for the EU".

Here is where the big problem unimaginably happened. Both France and the Netherlands decisively rejected it to the shocked disbelief and consternation of Brussels. This in theory and according to EU rules killed it stone dead. However, with the EU when you get the wrong answer, you just keep asking the question until you get the right answer on the basis that the misguided voters either didn't mean what they said or needed educating.

Firstly though, we tried to see who was lying to us and you can judge for yourself.

The leaders of France, Germany and Holland said outright that the new Lisbon Treaty to replace the rejected constitution was 95 to 99 per cent the same as before, with just superficial alterations in wording, and that any opt-outs secured by the then prime minister Tony Blair were not worth the paper they were written on, though in slightly more diplomatic language.

The British government stated that it was only another treaty, that it had got secure opt-outs on all the points it wanted and that because it did not pass more powers to Brussels there was no need for the referendum which they had promised.

So, cutting through the forest of verbiage, let us get down to particulars and try and see what our leaders proposed to give away.

As Ruth Lea says in her "Essential guide to the European Union", this constitutional Treaty is unlike any previous treaty for three main reasons:

The constitutional implications are profound.

There are major institutional changes.

There is an unprecedented transfer of powers to the EU.

The EU would have full legal personality, it would become a state. Its powers would no longer be based on treaties. Member states would cease being independent countries.

There would be an EU Head of State and Foreign Minister under whatever name. The EU Foreign Minister called the High Representative to avoid delicate British susceptibilities will preside over a single supranational diplomatic service. This will include seconded diplomats from member countries, but, they will be accountable to and owe their loyalty to, the new EU Foreign Office.

Also, member states will not necessarily know what is going on in negotiations between the EU and other governments. This is all in Working Paper No 28, EU Foreign Service.

Sixty vetoes would go and Qualified Majority Voting QMV would become the norm.

We would also become real instead of notional EU citizens and our loyalty and allegiance would be to the EU, not to our own country. This would not of course be spelt out in black and white, but this would be the effect.

The "treaty" also imposes a legal duty on parliaments "to contribute actively to the good functioning of the union", a catch-all phrase if ever there was one.

Even more important, the constitution would be an enabling one, so that where the Union has not yet got complete power it has "shared competence", where member countries can only act if the EU chooses not to.

One of these competences is "freedom, security and justice" and this is where "corpus juris" comes in which is even nastier than it sounds.

Also, as the constitution does not set limits to Union power, its powers would be effectively limitless, with the powers of the member states only those permitted by the Union. Even more deadly, powers are written in so that the constitution/treaty could be altered in future without all the democratic bother of setting up further treaties. This is under a new "simplified revision procedure" allowing incremental change.

The new union would have the constitutional status of statehood.

As some perceptive person wrote, this is the final stage of a slow moving *coup d'etat*.

Why then do I single out corpus juris from the long list of powers proposed to be given away to this power hungry monster?

I do so because it cuts at the heart of our ancient system of justice and freedom without which we are truly no longer free men and women.

I'll make it as simple as I can. Even at my advanced age I'd rather be doing other things than raising my blood pressure writing this.

Corpus Juris is a fully-fledged plan painstakingly prepared by the European Commission, as some perceptive writer said, pointing a loaded pistol at the heart of our most ancient liberties.

It first came to our notice when a student of Italian law called Torquil Dick Erickson was invited by mistake, having a non-English name, to a select gathering of "members of European Jurists for the protection of the financial interests of the Union". It was called to unveil the detailed project of Corpus Juris and was envisaged as the embryo of a future European criminal code. No English or Irish were invited.

The proposals were and still are:

A single legal area in the EU.

A European Public Prosecutor, with National Public Prosecutors "under a duty to assist him".

A Judge of Freedoms, straight from Orwell's 1984, a scary prophetic book which I've mentioned before. His job would merely be to ensure any arrest was lawful under Corpus Juris rules, not to demand evidence for arrest.

A European Arrest Warrant issued by any national judge on instructions from the European Public Prosecutor "means any national police force would be required to enforce it".

The arrested suspect could then be imprisoned for six months, renewable for any further number of three month periods, without any evidence being produced.

The eventual trial would be held by professional judges with none of the bother of having a jury or lay magistrates.

The prosecution could then retry a prisoner on appeal even after acquittal and continue this process, as opposed to our law of double jeopardy.

To remind you, in our law we have suspicion, investigation, arrest and charge.

In Europe the sequence is suspicion, ARREST and imprisonment, investigation and eventually charge.

Spell this path to tyranny out to any knowledgeable person today and they would laugh and say we would never accept it.

Unfortunately under Article 280 of the Amsterdam Treaty it can be introduced and we have no veto. It will be introduced in three easy stages to sugar the pill to the gullible British.

Stage 1 - It will just apply to the European Commission and their employees.

Stage 2 - A Prosecutor's office will be established in each state to work with police and law courts.

Stage 3 - After a period an intergovernmental conference will ratify the introduction of Corpus Juris and then establish a European Prosecutor's office.

This is the classic EU process: a secretive start, government and EU denials – "only a discussion paper", then legislation by stealth until it is too late to stop it.

I remind you that in the official memorandum to the Corpus Juris document it is described as "a fairer, simpler and more efficient system of repression". This seems a refreshingly accurate description.

Another definition of a police state which fits in with this is "where the police or paid servants of the state can arrest people and send them to prison without trial".

Back to the Constitution and cast your eyes down this list of "exclusive competences", i.e. complete power which the treaty would give the EU.

Before you do that though, consider this admission by one Guiliano Amato, a former Italian Prime Minister and one of the principle architects of the rejected constitution, in a speech given in London on the "Treaty" to replace it. "They (the EU leaders) decided that the document should be unreadable. If it is unreadable, it is not constitutional, that was the sort of perception. Should you succeed in understanding it at first sight there might be some reason for a referendum, because it would mean there was something new."

This was accomplished by putting the proposals in the

constitution into amendments to existing treaties and not publishing the consolidated 3,000 pages until the treaty had been ratified.

To resume, without further comment.

Competition rules for the functioning of the market.
Customs Union.
Monetary policy.
Marine and Biological resources.
The ability to sign treaties and agreements on the following:

Communications.
Public Health, which would tell your Mother and the NHS what to do and how to do it.
Energy.
Commercial Policy.
Criminal Justice.

So as not to miss anything out, the following would be "shared competences", the definition of shared being that nations could only legislate on them if the EU chose not to do so:

The Internal Market.
Freedom, Security and Justice.
Agriculture and Fisheries.
Transport and trans European networks.
Energy (a new competence).
Social policy.
Economic, social and territorial cohesion, Environment.
Consumer Protection.
Safety in public health matters.

It may occur to you that this lot doesn't leave a great deal for our well-paid 600-odd MPs in Westminster to chat about. This applies even more to SMPs in Edinburgh.

That however should not worry the EU Commission as long as they are left in place for people to vote them in and out of office periodically as a façade of democracy.

You will remember the following which were dealt with in Chapter Five but also come under the heading of vanishing freedom.

These include the growth of Europol with its new headquarters now to be established in Denmark, the European Gendarmerie Force with its Spanish and French associations and the unreported massive order for crowd-control weaponry for the Home Office, now presumably updated.

The process of eventually getting the whole population on a DNA database is currently gathering speed, with reports of police taking swabs for crimes as severe as dropping litter or speeding.

Anyone could be on it with details trawled by unknown officials and combined with those of real criminals on other EU country's data bases. There was also the linkage of national data bases EU-wide, done for bland and sensible sounding reasons.

Chapter Five also dealt with ID cards and sophisticated surveillance and the pressure of political correctness leading to self-censorship.

An idea the EU Commission is working on is for EU-wide political parties where those making the right noises would be subsidized. This comes from the Treaty of Nice, where an article states that "The Council....... shall lay down the regulations governing political parties at European level and in particular the rules regarding their funding".

It then goes on to say in Eurospeak that parties must agree with the objectives of the EU before they can be registered and that Article Four of the treaty lays down a process of verification of these obligations.

It then says that the European Parliament could de-register a party which "did not satisfy the conditions for registration".

You will immediately see that this would make it nearly impossible for any real opposition to survive and the heresy of opposition to the EU religion could in practice be banned.

Sun Tzu, a very wise and successful Chinese general some 2,500 years ago, wrote, "Those who make peaceful revolution impossible, make violent revolution inevitable".

That is very nearly enough doom and gloom for one chapter, except for two completely harmless sounding pieces of home grown legislation, entitled the "Civil Contingences Act, 2004", and the "Legislative and Regulatory Reform Bill".

The first gives the Prime Minister or Secretary of State or even a government whip, powers to repeal or amend any laws and to do practically whatever they like in an emergency. They could even extend the life of a parliament.

The second proposed legislation, on hold after being heavily challenged in the House of Lords, aims to give Ministers powers to alter any law without going back to Parliament, apart from where it increases taxation or where the penalty is more than two years in prison.

It is extraordinarily similar to the enabling act which gave Hitler the total power he gained in Nazi Germany in 1933.

It would certainly enable ministers to avoid uproar over unpopular edicts from Brussels. Again it is similar to the "enabling clause" in the proposed EU constitution which would have the same effect.

A widespread suggested alternative title for this last proposed legislation was "The Abolition of Parliament Bill".

9

The solution?

So what is the solution?

There are several interesting approaches to getting rid of the EU. A very interesting Russian, now British, called Vladimir Bukovsky, spent some forty years fighting communist dictatorship in and out of concentration camps so he is by way of being an expert in dealing with tyranny. Indeed he draws an interesting comparison between the Soviet dictatorship and the EU.

The Soviet Union dictatorship he says was governed by fifteen appointed people who were not accountable to anyone.

The EU is governed by two dozen appointed people not accountable to anyone and whom you cannot sack.

He also compares the ideological dictatorship of the communists with the statist ideology of "socialism for ever" in the EU and compares their similar "top down" corruption compared with normal corruption which starts at the bottom and works up.

My point from this, is that he is worth listening to on the subject of losing your freedom

He gave an address to a parliamentary group and discussed those who say keep in the EU and try and change it from the inside. He went on to quote an old Bolshevik, who suggested this as a way to alter the communist dictatorship. (The tape may one day be classed as subversive which will make it interesting.)

One of his comrades said this was like trying to cure a girl of a sexually-transmitted disease by sleeping with her. You won't cure her but you are very likely to catch it.

Interestingly he says "I lived in your future and I didn't like it". He says also that "you are in the process of losing your freedom, take it from me as an expert on that subject", but that if anyone can destroy the EU it will be the Poles.

He also encourages by making the point that the intellectuals in Brussels are not as ruthless as the old KGB Russian secret police who had to kill forty million people to keep the lid on communism. They're afraid of crowds, he says, but we will get no help from the main political parties. Only a mass grass-roots movement will defeat the EU.

A few ideas on this theme.

In America in 1849 just before the civil war, Henry David Thoreau wrote his famous essay on "Civil disobediance". Its basic theme was that in the face of unjust law it is not only the right but the duty of good men and women to resist such law.

The basic rules and requirements for civil disobediance were sensiby laid out by both Gandhi and Martin Luther King. These were:

1. A valid cause. Regaining our democratic freedom should cover that and perhaps for a start getting a referendum on the Lisbon Treaty (EU Constitution).

2. Large numbers, good leadership and strong organisations.

One inspiring leader could generate all this. Even a small beginning would grow on its own momentum once people saw it was becoming effective.

3. All initiatives must be non violent in all circumstances.

4. Generate victimless crimes and make it fun.

5. If there is a price for actions, it must not be paid by members of the public.

6. Any campaign should be totally inclusive getting the widest possible spectrum of support.

Perhaps such a campaign of civil disobediance would be the answer for the huge number of people, who, aware that whatever they vote for makes increasingly little difference, feel disenfranchised and helpless.

We could, of course, solve the whole problem in about twenty minutes by Parliament repealing the European Communities Act of 1972 thus making all the subsequent treaties null and void, including the circa 200,000 directives and regulations now afflicting us.

This sounds too easy but there is no legal impediment at all to our leaving. The government confirmed on 8th February 2007 that this is so, that Parliament could repeal the European Communities Act of 1972 and there are no provisions in any treaty which affect the ultimate ability of the United Kingdom to withdraw from the EU.

We would not be the first. Greenland, then a province of Denmark, left the EU in 1985 and has prospered.

Even the dreaded proposed EU Constitution says in article 1-60, under voluntary withdrawal from the Union, "....any member state may decide to withdraw from the union in accordance with its own constitutional requirements". This same draft requires the EU to "develop a special relationship with neighbouring countries ......and conclude specific agreements with the countries concerned". This appears to be opening an avenue for the breakup of the EU, though not perhaps what the people who drafted it envisaged.

However perhaps we should be cautious of EU promises. Jean Monnet, who we have met before, and if you can't remember you can look him up in the index, had other ideas in the 1950s, reprinted in his memoirs in 1978.

"The withdrawal of a state which has committed itself to the Community should be possible only if all the others agree to such withdrawal and the conditions in which it takes place."

All this talk of leaving is a happy thought but unlikely at present while all the main parties including Her Majesty's Loyal Opposition still intone the mantra that we must stay in the EU because of it's manifest advantages which have yet to be itemised or debated.

Going back to the excellent Mr Bukovsky, the EU he says will collapse when its actions start to affect the young, even if it's in built contradictions don't start the process first. This will probably be in the period 2010 to 2012 when the Lisbon Treaty (Constitution) starts to bite. If this sounds defeatist, consider that the EU Parliament voted in February 2008 by 499 votes to 129 not to respect the forthcoming vote of the Irish refererendum, which the Irish were obliged to have because of their constitution.

However, this was one political decision that the EU political class couldn't stich up and the Irish voted NO in June 2008 by a substantial majority (with a 53.13 per cent turnout) of 53.4 per cent to 46.6 per cent in spite of prophesis of doom from all their political parties and the media.

There was dismay and bewilderment in Brussels and unrestrained joy elsewhere especially in the UK who had been cheated of their referendum. According to EU rules the treaty was now dead.

In a gesture of lofty contempt for the peoples they ruled the President of the Commission then urged all the tame parliaments of the remaining twenty six countries, none of which had allowed a referendum, to continue ratifying the dead treaty. Our House of Lords, the revising chamber and last defender of liberties then voted to ratify the treaty so the Commons could do the same.

Meanwhile, any decision in a meeting in Brussels on how to resurrect the Treaty was postponed. The Commission and the flock of national Prime Ministers appeared still in shock, unable to decide how to respond to rejection.

The EU now appears to have a number of options.

It could ignore the vote completely as if the Irish didn't exist on the basis that they have been deluded or misled. However, a number of other smaller states particularly the Czechs, having escaped Communist dictatorship but not wanting to stick their necks out being new, appear to have suppressed doubts about the Treaty. But if the Irish could....?

Alternatively the Commission could tinker with the Treaty and try and persuade the Irish to vote again and get it right, a well tried and effective method in the past. However, there were many reasons for the rejection and it would be difficult to address them all. Also they might vote NO again.

Further if the Irish were granted concessions others might want them too.

Finally, and this is most probable, they will continue bringing in aspects of the Treaty/Constitution piecemeal as they were already doing in the gap between rejection of the original Constitution and its rebirth as the Lisbon Treaty.

One thing is quite certain.

The EU has learnt it's lesson and will make absolutely sure that they will never again run the risk of asking we the people what we think. That was called democracy.

Then again, once the Lisbon Treaty/Constitution is in force there will be no need for them to ask.

For the future Mr Hague, once leader of the Conservative Party, one of the main parties, refers to a poll which indicates a high degree of eurorealism in the young which is promising, and, certainly, when both sides of the EU is explained to schoolchildren in lectures, they vote strongly against it.

As to solutions, there is really only one, to unlock the cell door and quietly walk away.

For the present, if we the "subversives" cannot stir this country out of its present apathy, remember one final quotation from a French philosopher, "A society of sheep begets a government of wolves".

Postscript

This is addressed to my grandchildren and to all our grandchildren.

Having then had a comprehensive moan about our loss of freedom and how it happened, what did I personally do about it?

The answer is I suppose, a lot more than most, a tiny fraction of what many did and less than I could have done. I wrote lots of letters mostly published (your mother has been collecting them for the family archives) and joined every organisation that was fighting the EU that I could find.

I went to lots of meetings but it was all talking to the converted and I talked to friends and relations but, like most people, they were too comfortable, apathetic or convinced that if the BBC said it was a good thing what was the problem?

To sum up, (when you are of an age to read this):

If England is no longer on published maps but just nine regions of an off-shore province of a new European Empire, then you are living in a dictatorship.

If the Scottish Regional Parliament takes its orders and money from Brussels, then you are living in a dictatorship.

If the only political parties you can vote for are Pan-European parties approved by Brussels and criticism of the EU can be considered a crime, then you are living in a dictatorship.

If Corpus Juris is established instead of our traditional legal system and we no longer have trial by jury or habeas corpus and the English Common Law has been abandoned, then you are living in a dictatorship.

If our police forces are part of Europol, then you are living in a dictatorship.

If the press and television follow the Brussels line unflinchingly with no hint of criticism, then you are living in a dictatorship.

If our army is part of a European army and controlled by the EU, and the Royal Navy flies the EU stars instead of the white ensign, then you are living in a dictatorship.

If the compulsory National Syllabus extols the benefits of being in the EU, you will know the rest.

Finally, if all the laws that matter are still decided by unelected officials in Brussels, however apparently benign the process, you are no longer free, you are still living in a dictatorship.

My suggestion then would be that you have three choices. If they don't want to live under this system then you can emigrate to a country which is still free or stay and fight, but that could be a tough option.

Alternatively, being young, you can just bide your time and wait for the EU's internal contradictions and absurdities to make it implode. No reason why you can't give it a shove as the opportunity offers but be careful.

May I suggest finally that you read George Orwell's "1984" and possibly Andrew Robert's "The Aachen Memorandum". Robert's is an historian who was at Cambridge with your mother.

You can then judge how far your country has gone down the road.

Remember, that like the communist dictatorships, the EU always tries to avoid the democratic judgement of those it rules. When that judgement does come it will be merciless.

The end may be messy but being free again will work miracles.

Books

Atkinson, Rodney, McWhirter, Norris, "Treason at Maastricht", Computerprint, 1997.

Booker, Christopher, North, Richard, "The Great Deception Can the EU survive?" Continuum, 2004.

Booker, Christopher, North, Richard, "The Mad Officials", Constable, 1994.

Booker, Christopher, North, Richard, "The Castle of Lies", Duckworth and Co. 1996.

Baimbridge, Mark, Burkitt, Brian, Wyman, Philip, "Alternative Futures", CIB 2005.

Clark, Ross, "How to label a Goat", Harriman House.

Connolly, Bernard, "The Rotten Heart of Europe", Faber and Faber, 1995.

Coleman, Ve rnon, "England, our England" and "Saving England", Blue Books Pub. 2002.

Hilton, Adrian, "The Principality and Power of Europe", Dorchester House Pub. 1997.

Jenkins, Lindsay, "Britain held Hostage" and "Disappearing Britain," Orange State Press 1998 and 2005.

Lea, Ruth, "Essential Guide to the European Union", Center for Policy Studies, 2004.

Mote, Ashley, "Vigilance, A Defence of British Liberty", Tanner Pub. 2001.

Oborne, Peter, "The Triumph of the Political Class", Simon and Schuster, 2007.

Orwell, George, "Nineteen Eighty Four", Secker and Warburg, 1949.

Roberts, Andrew, "The Aachen Memorandum", Orion Books, 1996.

Sexton, Stuart, "A Guide to the Treaty establishing a Constitution for Europe", Pub. By The Education Unit, Warningham Park School, Warlinham, 2005.

"The Provisional Text of the Draft Treaty establishing a Constitution for Europe". The Foreign and Commonwealth Office. EU Directorate, 2004.

Pamphlets

Bruges Group, "Federalist Thought Control".
Bruges Group, "Free Speech, the EU Version", Dr Brian Hindley.
The Freedom Association, "Freedom or Tyranny".
The Freedom Association, "The Freedom Audit".
Heathcote – Amory, MP "The European Condition".
North, Richard, "Food Safety in the EU". Group Europe of Diversity and Democracy, (EDD) 2000.
Lord Pearson of Rannoch ,"What is the point of the European Union? Memorandum for opinion formers".
Redwood, John, "The Bad Bet", Research Centre Free Europe.
Redwood John, "101 Reasons for leaving the EU", St. Matthews Pub. Ltd.
Redwood John, "The European Project," Technographic Systems.
"EUSSR The Soviet roots of European integration". Vladimir Bukovsky and Pavel Stroilov, Sovereignty Publications.

Periodicals

"CIB Newsletters", Campaign for an Independent Brittain.
"*eurofacts*", The June Press.
"*European Journal*", The European Foundation.
"*Facts, Figures and Phantasies*", Christina Speight. London.
"*Freedom Today*", The Freedom Association.
"*The Flag*", BCM The Flag, London.
"*Independence Newsletter*", the United Kingdom Independence Party.
"*Notes from the Borderland*", issue 4, 2002.
"*Resistance*", New Alliance, London.
"*S.O.S. Save our Sovereignty*", Iris Binstead, Polruan by Fowey, Cornwall.

Better off Out Campaign
www.betteroffout.co.uk
British Declaration of Independence
www.bdicampaign.org
British Weights & Measures Assoc.
www.bwmaOnline.com
Bruges Group
www.brugesgroup.com
Campaign Against Euro-Federalism
www.caef.org.uk
Campaign for an Independent Britain
www.cibhq.co.uk
Democracy Movement
www.democracymovement.org.uk
EU Observer
www.euobserver.com
EU Truth
www.eutruth.org.uk
European Commission (London)
www.cec.org.uk
European Foundation
www.europeanfoundation.org
European No Campaign
www.europeannocampaign.com
Facts & Figures
www.eufactsfigures.com
Foreign Affairs
www.foreignaffairs.org
Freedom Association
www.tfa.net
Global Britain
www.globalbritain.org
Global Vision
www.global-vision.net
I Want a Referendum
www.iwantareferendum.com

June Press (Publications)
www.junepress.com
Labour Euro-Safeguards Campaign
www.lesc.org.uk
New Alliance
www.newalliance.org.uk
Open Europe
www.openeurope.org.uk
Regional Assemblies
www.regionalassemblies.co.uk
Speak Out Campaign
www.speakout.co.uk
Sovereignty
www.sovereignty.org.uk
Statewatch
www.statewatch.org
The People's "No" Campaign
www.thepeoplesnocampaign.co.uk
United Kingdom Independence Party
www.ukip.org

INDEX